THE BEST
W●NES
IN THE
S●PER
MARKE●S
2020

NED HALLEY

D1440256

foulsham
LONDON • NEW YORK • TORONTO • SYDNEY

W. Foulsham & Co. Ltd

for Foulsham Publishing Ltd

The Old Barrel Store, Drayman's Lane, Marlow, Bucks SL7 2FF

Foulsham books can be found in all good bookshops and direct from www.foulsham.com

ISBN: 978-0-572-04794-8

Text copyright © 2019 Ned Halley
Series, format and layout design © 2019 Foulsham Publishing

Cover photographs © Thinkstock

A CIP record for this book is available from the British Library

The moral right of the author has been asserted

Printed and bound in Great Britain by Martins the Printers Ltd

Contents

—How to choose?—

Too much choice. It's become an everyday complaint about supermarket shopping. A first world problem, as we now say. It's real enough. Aldi and Lidl have done as well out of limiting choice as they have from cutting prices.

Who saw that coming? Not the giant grocery multiples, who have only very lately started to rationalise their offerings. That's after years of trying to compete for customers through very little more than noisily advertised discounting.

Wine shoppers have certainly benefitted along the way. We have been offered vast choices from all around the world at prices kept to an absolute minimum, reduced even further by perpetual promotions. It's helped make Britain a 'wine-drinking nation' and of course broadened the range of wines on offer. No other country gets the choice we do.

That's as much the business of the traditional wine trade as it is of the supermarkets. It's true that the supermarkets annihilated the old off-licence chains, but long-established independent merchants have proved remarkably resilient, and new one-off wine shops, as well as online outfits, are popping up everywhere, extending choice into every imaginable wine style as well as from every producing region.

In the realm of wine, supermarkets will no doubt continue to compete more with each other than they will with specialist merchants, and that's fine. But there's clearly a future in supermarket wine, and it starts here.

All the big supermarkets, with the notable exception of Waitrose, have been trimming their wine ranges. Asda lately chopped 25 per cent off its range in one go and the Tesco list looks half the length of just a few years back. Definitely less choice. But besides a few mourned old favourites, I can't say the fall in numbers materially alters the appeal of the ranges.

This year, by which I mean 2019, followed a very productive 2018 harvest across Europe, and the rest of the world continued to overproduce as usual. There's no shortage of wine. And I cannot recall a tasting season that has offered so many genuinely interesting and sensibly priced wines from the supermarkets. For all the excitement over climate change, economic chaos and bloody Brexit, I reckon supermarket-wine shoppers have never had it so good.

I have certainly never before awarded so many top scores in any one edition of *The Best Wines in the Supermarkets* – here in its seventeenth successive year – with a total of 41, and more than 100 making 9 points out of ten.

The stability of prices in the context of currency fluctuation and taxation is remarkable. Given that virtually all our wine is imported (*pace* the English and Welsh vineyards), the pound's periodical lapses seem to leave prices unperturbed. In February 2019 the new excise duty levels announced in our first autumn Budget were imposed, but I don't recall any adjustments at all. The duty on a bottle of still wine rose from £2.60 to £2.68 (including VAT) and on sparkling from £3.32 to £3.43. That the supermarkets are able to offer as many decent wines below £6 or even £5 as they continue to do is even more of a mystery than ever. But they do, and at no apparent cost to quality.

At all price levels, Spain is shining particularly brightly at the moment. Rioja leads the way. Tesco and Waitrose are both good sources, and Marks & Spencer have a very alluring new range from the region. Morrisons are offering not just a top-drawer Gran Reserva red but an unreconstructed oxidative white of a kind I had feared extinct.

It's a fair point that the supermarkets do make it their business to offer wines in a fairly set number of categories and classes. You can expect to find currently fashionable lines in just about every retailer. Every Italian range will include a Gavi as well as a Soave, a Pecorino or a Primitivo as well as a Pinot Grigio. Spanish ranges now always encompass a Rias Baixas Albariño and very often a Rueda Verdejo. From France, you're as guaranteed to find a Picpoul de Pinet as a Muscadet, a Châteauneuf du Pape (however outrageous the price) as a Côtes du Rhône.

So what if it's predictable? Confronted with the serried ranks on the wine shelves, it's a proper comfort to find familiar names. Far better than too much choice.

Still on the matter of choice I must explain why the retailers included in *The Best Wines in the Supermarkets 2020* are fewer by two than in the previous edition. I have dropped Majestic. I must finally concede the point that the warehouse chain is not a supermarket, and following its 2019 sale to a Japanese bank it faces alterations. I await developments.

The absence of Spar, following its debut last year, will I hope be remedied in a future edition. I have not had the chance to taste a significant number of new vintages, or new wines. I hope to revisit the Spar range soon.

The upside is that I have room for more wines from each of the big players. There are more than 500 wines here altogether and I commend just about all of them. As usual I have allocated each wine a score out of ten, and all but a very few are rated 8 or upwards. Those scoring 8 are unconditionally recommended as good of their kind and fair value. At 9 I am implying very good of their kind and very good value too, and top-scoring wines are those I reckon are exceptional in both respects.

You might not always think my scores are always consistent with the descriptions or even the tone of the descriptions. This is because my points system is in a way independent of my ramblings. I write down the score based entirely on the likeability/price ratio. The number is instinctive, as I stand there with the glass in hand and the price in mind. I never change the score later. It's about first impressions. And first impressions count for a lot when you're tasting great numbers of wines, one after the other.

Taste in wine, I hardly need to add, is personal to each of us. My descriptions and points system are wholly subjective, but I hope helpful and enlightening. On the day, of course, the choice is yours.

Where does the best wine come from?

It's France, I suppose. Fabled estates in Bordeaux, Burgundy and Champagne have a perpetual monopoly on the most-venerated red, white and sparkling wines, worldwide. If your budget per bottle starts at £100 I guess that's all you need to know. But for those of us who buy wine in supermarkets and consider even £10 a bit of a punt, the question needs to be readdressed.

In the global context, you could argue that the country of origin of any wine is immaterial. But the supermarkets wouldn't agree with you. They arrange all the wines in their stores and on their websites precisely according to their nationality.

It's quite odd. You wouldn't display your canned fruits and vegetables this way, would you? Or your frozen fish? Or anything else, really? But that's the way they do the wine and, accordingly, that's the way I arrange the listings in this book.

To be fair, the wines of particular nations and regions do have identifiable attributes even when made from a common grape variety. The white wines from fashionable Sauvignon Blanc, for example, have distinct styles at home in France's Loire Valley and away in the Marlborough region of New Zealand. Chilean Sauvignon has its own qualities, and so does South African.

Germany, though never in fashion, makes inimitably delicious wines from the Riesling grape. Australian wines from this noble variety are so different that I suspect uninitiated devotees of the Mosel and Rhine would hardly recognise a Clare Valley Riesling at all.

While the grape does much to determine the nature of the wine, location still counts for a lot. Landscape and soil conditions, weather and the peculiar skills and customs of the winemakers all have their parts to play.

The French have a word for it: *terroir*, which loosely translates as 'soil', but *vignerons* in France take it to mean the entirety of conditions local to the site of crop production. That's not just the soil but the lie of the land, its geographical position, its climate and indeed what the tillers of that soil and the custodians of the crops get up to.

On visits to France, I have heard much of terroir. Amid the most-valued vineyards of Chablis I have learned that the ground is composed largely of oyster shells, mountainised over millennia into vertiginous slopes. From these bleak, frost-ravaged heights come some of the world's most minerally luscious dry white wines. I've had it all endlessly explained to me and never really understood, but be in no doubt: *grand cru* Chablis is like no other wine.

And so on across all of France. Elsewhere, winemakers might not speak of terroir, but they all believe in the real or imagined unique properties of their estates. They all consider their wines to be an expression of their locations and traditions. This is what gives wine its much-treasured diversity, and of course its mystique. Wine is more than a mere nutritious drug. It's part natural phenomenon, part art form. Hurrah to that, I say.

It's all about the
grape variety

The grape, naturally, counts for everything in wine. The finished product is, after all, simply the fermented juice of the fruit. Well, yes, there will be a cultured yeast introduced to assist the process. And there are permitted additives, mostly sulphur products and clarifying agents, to ensure healthy, bright wine. The wine's natural sugars and acids can be supplemented.

But the grape variety still sets the pace. Dark-skinned grapes make red wine because the skins are included in the must (pressed juice) during fermentation and give the wine its colour. The juice of virtually all grapes is clear. You can make white wine with dark-skinned grapes by extracting the juice promptly and fermenting it free of the skins. The base wine for Champagne is made largely from dark-skinned grapes. But still white wine is made much more simply – from pale-skinned grapes fermented without their skins.

Different grape varieties produce correspondingly different wines. There are hundreds of distinct varieties, but a couple of dozen account for most production. All of us have favourites, or at least preferences. The varieties described here account for most of the wines on offer in the supermarkets.

Red wine varieties

Aglianico: Ancient variety of southern Italy said to have been imported by immigrant Greek farmers around

500 BC. The name is a recent rendering of former Ellenico ('Hellenic') and the grape has caught on again thanks to Aglianico del Vulture, a volcanic DOC of Basilicata. The wines are dark, intense, pungent and long-lived.

Barbera: The most widely planted dark-skinned grape of Piedmont in northwest Italy makes easy-drinking purple vigorous rasping red wine to enjoy young and also, increasingly, a darker, denser but still vigorous style given gravitas through oak-ageing. Mostly sold under denominations Barbera d'Asti and Barbera d'Alba. Unrelated to Barbaresco, a Piedmontese wine made from Nebbiolo grapes.

Cabernet Sauvignon: Originally of Bordeaux and the mainstay of claret, Cabernet berries are compact and thick-skinned, making wine of intense flavour and gripping tannin. The grandest wines need decades to develop their full bloom. Everyday wines made worldwide typically have dense colour, purple in youth, aromas of blackcurrants and cedar wood ('cigar box') and firm, juicy-savoury fruit.

Gamay: It's the grape of Beaujolais. Colour can be purple with a blue note; nose evokes new-squashed raspberries with perhaps a pear drop or two, the effect of carbonic maceration, the Beaujolais method of vinification. Fruit flavours are juicy, bouncing, even refreshing.

Grenache: The French name for the Garnacha, originally of Spain, where it is much employed in Rioja and other classic regions. HQ in France is the southern Rhône Valley with further widespread plantings across the country's Mediterranean regions. Wines can be light in colour but emphatic in flavour with a wild, hedgerow-fruit style lifted with spice and pepper. Widely cultivated across the New World.

Malbec: The signature grape of Argentina. A native of Bordeaux, where it plays a minor blending role, it thrives in the high-altitude vineyards of Mendoza, a province of the Andean foothills. The best wines have dark colour and a perfume sometimes fancifully said to evoke leather and liquorice; flavours embrace briary black fruits with suggestions of bitter chocolate, plum and spice.

Merlot: Bordeaux variety very often partnering Cabernet Sauvignon in claret blends and also solo in fabled Pomerol wines including Château Petrus. The grape is large and thin-skinned compared to Cabernet, making wine of rich ruby colour with scents evoking black cherry and cassis and fruit that can be round and rich. Ordinary wines are soft, mellow and early developing but might lack the firmness of tannin that gives balance.

Pinot Noir: It's the solo grape of red burgundy and one of three varieties in champagne. Everyday Pinot wines typically have a bright, translucent ruby colour and aromas evoking red soft summer fruits and cherries. Flavours correspond. Fine Pinot has elegant weight and shape, mysteriously alluring. New Zealand makes distinctive, delicious, sinewy Pinots; Chile produces robust and earthy Pinots; California's best Pinots compare for quality with fabulously expensive Burgundies.

Sangiovese: The grape of Chianti, so-named after the Latin for 'the blood of Jove', makes pleasingly weighted, attractively coloured wines with plummy perfume, even pruny in older wines, and slinky flavours evoking blackcurrant, raspberry and occasionally nectarine. Good Chianti always has a clear tannic edge, giving the wine its trademark nutskin-dry finish.

Syrah: At home in southern France, the Syrah makes wines that at their best are densely coloured, rich in aromas of sun-baked blackberries, silky in texture and plumply, darkly, spicily flavoured. The grandest pure-Syrah wines, such as Hermitage and Côte Rôtie, are gamey, ripe and rich and very long-lived. Syrah is widely planted across Mediterranean France as a blending grape in wines of the Côtes du Rhône and Languedoc. Under the name Shiraz, Syrah is Australia's most prolific red-wine variety.

Tempranillo: The grape at the heart of Rioja has to work hard. The unique selling point of the region's famous red wines is the long ageing process in oak casks that gives the finished product its creamy, vanilla richness – which can all too easily overwhelm the juiciness and freshness of the wine. The Tempranillo's bold blackcurranty-minty aromas and flavours stand up well to the test, and the grape's thick skin imparts handsome ruby colour that doesn't fade as well as firm tannins that keep the wine in shape even after many years in cask or bottle. Tempranillo is widely planted throughout Spain, and in Portugal, under numerous assumed names.

White wine varieties

Albariño: Rightly revered Iberian variety once better known in its Minho Valley, Portugal, manifestation as Alvarinho, a mainstay of vinho verde wine. Since the 1980s, Albariño from Spain's Galicia region, immediately north of Portugal, has been making aromatic and scintillatingly racy sea-fresh dry white wines from vineyards often planted close to the Atlantic shore. The seaside DO of Rias Baixas, now a major centre for gastro-tourism, is the heart of Albariño country. The variety, characterized by small, thick-skinned berries with many pips, is now also cultivated in California, New Zealand and beyond.

Chardonnay: Universal variety still at its best at home in Burgundy for simple appley fresh dry wines all the way up to lavish new-oak-fermented deluxe appellations such as Meursault and Montrachet making ripe, complex, creamy-nutty and long-developing styles. Imitated in Australia and elsewhere with mixed success.

Chenin Blanc: Loire Valley variety cultivated for dry, sweet and sparkling white wines, some of them among France's finest. Honeyed aromas and zesty acidity equally characterize wines including elegant, mineral AOP Vouvray and opulent, golden late-harvested AOP Coteaux du Layon. In South Africa, Chenin Blanc now makes many fascinating and affordable wines.

Fiano: Revived southern Italian variety makes dry but nuanced wines of good colour with aromas of orchard fruit, almonds and candied apricots and finely balanced fresh flavours. Fleetingly fashionable and worth seeking out.

Glera: Widely planted in the Veneto region of northeast Italy, it's the principal variety in prosecco sparkling wine. The grape itself used to be named prosecco, after the winemaking village of Prosecco near Treviso, but under a 2009 change to the wine-denomination rules, the name can now be applied exclusively to the wine, not the grape. Glera makes a neutral base wine with plenty of acidity. It is a prolific variety, and needs to be. Sales of prosecco in Britain have now surpassed those of champagne.

Palomino Fino: The grape that makes sherry. The vines prosper in the *albariza*, the sandy, sun-bleached soil of Andalucia's Jerez region, providing a pale, bone-dry base wine ideally suited to the sherry process. All proper sherry of every hue is white wine from Palomino Fino. The region's other grape, the Pedro Ximenez, is used as a sweetening agent and to make esoteric sweet wines.

Pinot Grigio: At home in northeast Italy, it makes dry white wines of pale colour and frequently pale flavour too. The mass-market wines' popularity might owe much to their natural low acidity. The better wines are aromatic, fleetingly smoky and satisfyingly weighty in the manner of Pinot Gris made in the French province of Alsace. New Zealand Pinot Gris or Pinot Grigio follows the Alsace style.

Riesling: Native to Germany, it makes unique wines pale in colour with sharp-apple aromas and racy, sleek fruit whether dry or sweet according to labyrinthine local winemaking protocols. Top-quality Rhine and Mosel Rieslings age wonderfully, taking on golden hues and a fascinating 'petrolly' resonance. Antipodean Rieslings have more colour and weight often with a mineral, limey twang.

Sauvignon Blanc: Currently fashionable thanks to New Zealand's inspired adoption of the variety for assertive, peapod-nettle-seagrass styles. Indigenous Sauvignons from France's Loire Valley have rapidly caught up, making searingly fresh wines at all levels from generic Touraine up to high-fallutin' Sancerre. Delicate, elegant Bordeaux Sauvignon is currently on top form too.

Semillon: Along with Sauvignon Blanc, a key component of white Bordeaux, including late-harvested, golden sweet wines such as Sauternes. Even in dry wines, colour ranges up to rich yellow, aromas evoke tropical fruits and honeysuckle, exotic flavours lifted by citrus presence. Top Australian Semillons rank among the world's best.

Viognier: Formerly fashionable but perpetually interesting variety of the Rhône Valley makes white wines of pleasing colour with typical apricot aroma and almondy-orchardy fruit; styles from quite dry to fruitily plump.

More about these varieties and many others in 'A wine vocabulary' starting on page 158.

Brand awareness

Big-brand wines such as Blossom Hill and Hardy do not crowd the pages of this book. I do get to taste them, and leave most of them out. I believe they don't measure up for quality, interest or value.

The best wines in the supermarkets are very often own-brands. Own-brands date back to the 1970s, when interest in wine finally began to take root in Britain. Sainsbury's was first, with its own Claret, about 1975. It was hardly a revolutionary idea. Grand merchants like Berry Bros & Rudd (est 1698) had been doing own-label Bordeaux and much else besides, for ever.

In the supermarket sector, wine was bought on the wholesale market like anything else, from butter to washing powder. Only when interest in wine started to extend beyond the coterie served by the merchants did the mass retailers take any notice. It was thanks, of course, to the new craze for foreign travel, and to the good influence of writers like Elizabeth David, who revealed the joys of Continental-style food and drink. In 1966, Hugh Johnson's brilliant and accessible book *Wine* piqued the public consciousness as never before.

The adoption of supermarket wine was slow enough, but accelerated in the 1980s by the arrival of new, decent wines from Australia. Earlier on, cheap Aussie wines had been overripe, stewed rubbish, but breakthrough technology now enabled fresh, bold reds and whites of a different stripe. Wretched Europlonk brands like Hirondelle retreated before a tide of lush Chardonnay and 'upfront' Shiraz.

The horizon for supermarket wine buyers, always shackled by price constraint, was suddenly widened. In spite of the delivery distances, southern hemisphere producers could match their Old World counterparts for value as well as interest and quality.

In time, the winemakers of Europe fought back. Top estates carried on with 'fine wine' production, but humbler enterprises had to learn how to master real quality at the everyday level. They did. I believe the huge improvements in the simpler wines of the Continent owe much to the need to match the competition from the New World.

By the 1990s, Britain had become the world's biggest wine importer. Supermarkets were largely responsible, and now had muscle in the market. They started to dispatch their own people to vineyards and wineries worldwide, not just to buy the wines but to participate in their production. And always, they demanded the lowest-possible prices.

And so to today's proliferation of supermarket own-brands. They are the flagships of every one of the big grocers, and usually the focal point of promotions. They are, naturally enough, the wines of which their begetters are most proud. Mass-market brands do still persist in the supermarkets. Some are very good. I think of Blason, Chasse and Vieille Ferme from France; Baron de Ley and Miguel Torres from Spain; McGuigan and Penfolds from Australia; Catena from Argentina and Concha y Toro from Chile, among others.

If you have a favourite popular brand, do check the index to this book on page 188. It might not be mentioned in the entry for the supermarket where you're used to finding it, but that doesn't mean I've left it out.

──A *very good year*──

Until the last chosen wine is typed in, I have very little idea whether it's been a vintage year for *The Best Wines in the Supermarkets*. Well, this one has been. I have lavished maximum points on no fewer than 41 individual wines from among the couple of thousand tasted over the year. This is more than ever before. Maybe I am becoming more generously inclined, but it's more likely there are simply greater numbers of special wines out there. Why wouldn't there be?

Totting up the numbers, which is always fun, I find that France is first among the producers this year, as usual, with 14 top-scoring wines. Next is Italy with 8, followed by Argentina and Spain with 4 apiece and 3 each for Germany, Portugal and South Africa. Australia has 1, and so does England. At last.

More predictably perhaps, Waitrose comes out on top with 8 maximums. But the Co-op, Morrisons and Tesco are right behind, each with 7. Sainsbury's collects 6 and Marks & Spencer 4. Aldi and Asda have 1 apiece.

Red wines

Raoul Clerget Beaujolais 2018	Morrisons	£5.00
Tesco Douro 2017	Tesco	£5.75
The Best Barbera d'Asti 2016	Morrisons	£6.50
Solato Lambrusco	Asda	£6.50
Hereford Tempranillo 2018	Co-op	£7.00
Taste the Difference South African Pinotage 2018	Sainsbury's	£7.50
The Best Languedoc 2016	Morrisons	£7.75
Waitrose Blueprint Mendoza Malbec 2018	Waitrose	£7.99
Domaine des Ormes Saumur 2016	Co-op	£8.00
Molise Biferno Riserva 2014	Co-op	£8.00
The Best Toscana 2017	Morrisons	£8.25
Taste the Difference Morador Malbec 2018	Sainsbury's	£8.50
Finest Minervois La Livinière 2016	Tesco	£9.00
Helderburg Winery Cabernet Sauvignon 2017	M&S	£9.00
M Chapoutier Côtes du Rhône Villages 2018	Tesco	£9.00
Vinalba Finca La 70 Malbec Cabernet 2017	Co-op	£9.00

Terre de Faiano Primitivo 2017	Waitrose	£9.99
El Duque de Miralta Rioja Crianza 2015	M&S	£10.00
Château Tour de Gilet 2016	Waitrose	£10.99
Côtes du Rhône Guigal 2015	Waitrose	£11.99
The Best Rioja Gran Reserva 2012	Morrisons	£12.00
Taste the Difference Les Bouysses Cahors 2016	Sainsbury's	£13.00

White wines

JJ Prüm Riesling 2018	Aldi	£5.99
Finest St Mont 2017	Tesco	£6.50
Klein Street Grenache Blanc 2018	Morrisons	£6.50
Soave Classico 2018	M&S	£7.00
Vanita Grillo 2018	Co-op	£7.00
Taste the Difference Côtes du Rhône Blanc 2018	Sainsbury's	£8.00
Réserve du Boulas Côtes du Rhône Villages 2018	M&S	£10.00
Taste the Difference Greco di Tufo 2017	Sainsbury's	£10.00
Finest Yarra Valley Chardonnay 2017	Tesco	£11.00

Château de Montfort Vouvray 2017	Waitrose	£11.99
Reichsgraf von Kesselstatt Riesling Spätlese 2016	Co-op	£12.00
The Best Rioja Blanca Reserva 2015	Morrisons	£13.00
Willi Haag Brauneberger Juffer Riesling Auslese 2016	Waitrose	£19.99

Fortified wines

Waitrose Medium Dry Amontillado Sherry	Waitrose	£7.29
Finest 10-Year-Old Tawny Port	Tesco	£12.50
Sandeman 20-Year-Old Tawny Port	Waitrose	£39.99

Sparkling wines

Balfour 1503 Foxwood Cuvee	Co-op	£17.50
Sainsbury's Blanc de Noirs Champagne Brut	Sainsbury's	£19.00
Finest Premier Cru Champagne Brut	Tesco	£20.00

Aldi

Unassuming is the word, I suppose. Aldi stores are functional and devoted to value. Choice is limited: maybe 2,000 different lines on offer in your local outlet. A Big Four rival might have ten times that number.

So what does this signify for the wines? The range is certainly compact, and focused on budget buys, but that's not the whole story. While other mass retailers are reducing their ranges quite radically, Aldi's wines are multiplying and adding more quality. As other supermarkets (including Asda, Morrisons and Tesco) close down their dedicated online wine services, Aldi has an online wine shop and now even a members' wine club.

In short, Aldi is following its own path, heedless of the reductive policies of the competition. And Aldi counts. In 2020, it opens its 1,000th UK store. It has lately overtaken Waitrose and the Co-op to rank fifth for sales among all the supermarkets.

I have picked out nearly 50 wines, representing quite a large proportion of the offering. Spanish wines are impressive, including the stalwart Toro Loco range of extreme bargains. Italian reds are interesting and Australia has produced some fine surprises.

My number one pick is from Germany, an everyday Riesling from a great Mosel producer, JJ Prüm, at just £5.99. It's good and it begs a question: more to come from the fatherland, Aldi?

RED WINES

ARGENTINA

🍷 **8** **Exquisite Collection Argentinian Malbec 2018** £6.29

Sweetly plump and appealingly priced barbecue wine with friendly roasty ripeness and proper Malbec sinewy pungency; 13.5% alcohol.

🍷 **8** **Exquisite Collection Organic Malbec 2018** £6.99

Deep, bright purple colour and spicy black fruit with a bit of creaminess; 14.5% alcohol. Decent Mendoza red unrelated to the wine above.

🍷 **8** **Don Tomas Terroir Selection Malbec 2018** £7.99

Upscale oak-smoothed blackberry (even loganberry according to my speculative note) steak red which is worth the extra money and trim at the finish; 14% alcohol.

🍷 **8** **Lot Series Finca La Pampa Pinot Noir 2017** £9.99

From the excellent but diminishing Lot Series of premium wines, a pale but resolute Pinot with fresh strawberry notes and a nice dollop of oaky creaminess; 13.5% alcohol.

AUSTRALIA

🍷 **8** **Exquisite Collection South Australia Shiraz 2018** £5.79

Barbecue red – obvs – but this is cheap Aussie Shiraz with plenty of spicy bite as well as the expected woof (14.5% alcohol); dark, ripe and wholesome.

🍷 **8** **Ringleader Old Vine Grenache 2018** £5.99

Unexpectedly pale colour but a firmly flavoursome hedgerow-fruit Riverland party red you might like to try chilled; 14.5% alcohol.

RED WINES

CHILE

🍷 8 **Quisco Malbec 2018** £6.99
The lurid ruby-purple colour is belied by the rounded savoury fruit; nice grippy finish; 14% alcohol. This is a much better buy than its odd-tasting Merlot counterpart.

FRANCE

🍷 8 **Eugene Serrignon Bouches du Rhône 2018** £4.99
From the Mediterranean estuary of the Rhône, an early indicator that 2018 is a special vintage in the region: bloomingly ripe red fruit flavours with typical spice and tannin firmness; 14% alcohol.

🍷 9 **Beaujolais Villages 2018** £5.99
This betokens a bumper 2018 vintage in Beaujolais – juicy, bouncy, refreshingly keen uniquely characterful red to drink cool; 13% alcohol.

🍷 8 **Ferrandière Merlot 2018** £5.99
Labelled like a smart château-bottled claret this is a slick and grippy Languedoc pure Merlot with developed black-cherry fruit; 13.5% alcohol.

🍷 9 **Château Jean Gue Cuvée La Rose
Lalande de Pomerol 2015** £11.99
On sale online only and no doubt in limited supply this is nevertheless a wine to seek out if you enjoy serious claret. Already browning in colour it smells and tastes as elegantly evolved as it looks, offering up all the sleek and luxuriant fruits of right-bank Bordeaux in its prime; 13.5% alcohol and a snip at this price.

ITALY

🍷 8 **The Fire Tree Nero d'Avola 2018** £4.99
This credible Sicilian pasta red from an indigenous grape is an appassimento, made with a bit of must from concentrated grapes, adding heft to the plummy, earthy fruit; 13% alcohol.

RED WINES

ITALY

🍷 9 **Nero di Troia 2016** £5.99

Amiable briary Puglia wine merging plumptious blackberry ripeness with perky pungent cherry brightness to make an immediately appealing match for pasta, pizza, anything that needs a 'cut' of acidity; 13.5% alcohol. Makes an impression.

🍷 9 **Primanero Organic Primitivo 2016** £7.99

The deep ruby colour is browning and you get an agreeable tea note above the rich black fruit on the nose; complex plum, briar and herbaceous flavours follow up in the dark fruit and the finish is very trim; 14% alcohol.

🍷 8 **The Fire Tree Riserva 2013** £7.99

Meaningfully mature Sicilian blend of local Nero d'Avola with Syrah and Merlot which brings a warming spiciness to the intense savoury fruit; 14% alcohol.

PORTUGAL

🍷 8 **GYM Dão Red 2017** £5.69

Reassuring dense crimson colour telling of the Port grapes in this blend; it's plump, peppery and clovey in the approved Portuguese manner and attractively distinctive; 13% alcohol.

SPAIN

🍷 9 **Toro Loco Superior 2017** £3.99

Pale-coloured 'entry-level' plonk from prolific Utiel-Requena region with spiced redcurrant/cassis fruit of generous weight and trim balance; 12.5% alcohol. Cheapest and best of the Toro Loco reds.

RED WINES

SPAIN

🍷 8 **Big Gun Spanish Red** £5.49

I guess the name commemorates CS Forester's stirring novel of the Peninsular War, *The Gun*, in which Spanish guerillas triumph over evil French occupiers. Don't recoil: this non-vintage, brightly crimson Syrah-Tempranillo blend fires up nicely with spicy black flavours and a firm grip; 14.5% alcohol.

🍷 8 **Antiguo Barrel Aged Spanish Red 2014** £5.89

Plausible perfectly wholesome Rioja-style pure Tempranillo from Castille; pale to look at but well-endowed with vanilla-toned blackcurrant fruit; 13.5% alcohol.

🍷 8 **El Somo Rioja Reserva 2014** £12.99

Only available online, a well-made vanilla-sweet but vigorously ripe and silky grown-up Rioja at a price; 13.5% alcohol.

🍷 8 **Plow & Press Californian Pinot Noir 2018** £7.99

Crunchy bright cherry-strawberry sunnily ripe Monterey Pinot of impressive poise and purity; it's an elegant wine to drink with white meats and well-flavoured fish dishes; 13% alcohol.

USA

🍷 9 **Stave & Steel Bourbon Aged Cabernet Sauvignon 2015** £8.99

Rather grand and expensive claret-like perfume from this nicely mature Californian blend (part Merlot and Petite Syrah) is followed up by satisfying, poised and long-flavoured corresponding fruit; 13.5% alcohol. A convincing contrivance, mercifully with no suggestion of bourbon whiskey.

PINK WINES

 S de la Sablette Côtes du Luberon
Rosé 2018 £6.49
Attractive shell-pink colour, delicate strawberry nose and crunchy red-fruit juiciness in this inoffensive Provence party piece; 13% alcohol.

 Fleur de Prairie Côte de Provence
Rosé 2018 £7.69
Smart package for this pale and lively florally scented Mediterranean wine; delicate summery red-fruit flavours in elegant balance, convincingly fresh; 13% alcohol.

FRANCE

 Toro Loco Rosé 2018 £3.99
The magenta colour and sweet strawberry nose on this unsubtle party pink from Valencia are good predictors of the fullness of the fruit. It's quite dry in the end with an almost tart acidity and 12% alcohol, and it is very cheap.

SPAIN

WHITE WINES

SIA Australian Gewürztraminer
Riesling 2018 £5.99
Inspired Riverina blend combining the spicy-lychee pungency of the Gewürz with the racy apple-lemon lift of the Riesling; distinctive exotic dry wine of genuine character; 12% alcohol.

Exquisite Collection Clare Valley
Riesling 2018 £6.99
This dependable big limey dry food white (matches just about everything) has raciness and long sleek minerality; it has featured at the same price since Aldi was first included here in 2015; 11.5% alcohol.

AUSTRALIA

WHITE WINES

9 **Quisco Sauvignon Blanc 2018** £5.99
Unexpectedly for a Chilean Sauvignon, this anyday wine has emphatic asparagus notes and long, limey-grassy lush green fruit flavours; my pick of all the Aldi Sauvignons on the day; 13% alcohol.

7 **Exquisite Collection Lyme Block English Wine 2018** £9.99
Bravo Aldi for this patriotic adoption, but it's an entirely ordinary dry wine, green with tart acidity, at an unrealistic price; 12.5% alcohol.

8 **Exquisite Collection Touraine Sauvignon Blanc 2018** £5.89
Keen river-fresh grassy Loire Valley extra-dry wine is in the proper Sauvignon tradition and safely short of green; 12% alcohol.

8 **Exquisite Collection Marsanne 2018** £5.99
Tropical fruits and blanched nuts make fleeting appearances in this perky dry Languedoc white; it somehow seemed more Italian than French; 13% alcohol.

8 **Ferrandière Pinot Gris 2018** £5.99
Unusual Languedoc dry wine (Pinot Gris is little grown outside Alsace) majoring on white-fruit freshness, but with an agreeable memory of the grape's smoky spiciness; 13% alcohol.

8 **Vue Sur Mer Côte de Thau 2018** £5.99
Decidedly seaside theme to this pretend Picpoul from the shores of the Thau lagoon near the Mediterranean port of Sète; you get fresh tangy flavours, a suggestion of salinity, and a welcome lemony edge; 12% alcohol.

WHITE WINES

🍷 **8** **Exquisite Collection Picpoul de Pinet £6.49**   **£6.49**

This fashionable Mediterranean oyster-matcher has the expected zest and freshness with a good lick of sunny ripeness to the orchardy-citrus white fruits; 12.5% alcohol.

🍷 **10** **JJ Prüm Riesling 2018**   **£5.99**

JJ Prüm is among the great winemaking names of the Mosel, and this is undoubtedly one of the estate's humbler offerings, a bracingly keen almost colourless granny-smith-crisp aperitif wine of lovely purity, fermented out at 11.5% alcohol without residual sweetness. It gets top marks because it's here at Aldi at a good price – and maybe an augur that this German retailer might start offering us more of these home-grown marvels.

🍷 **8** **The Fire Tree Sicilian Fiano 2018**   **£4.99**

Straight bright island varietal shows herbaceous warmth within the orchard-fruit freshness; 13% alcohol.

🍷 **8** **Pianeta Organico Pinot Grigio 2018**   **£5.99**

Novelty pot-shape bottle delivers a pleasingly ripe but briskly dry and gently smoky-spicy variation on the eternal PG theme; 12% alcohol.

🍷 **8** **Gavi di Gavi 2018**   **£6.99**

Trendy Piedmont dry wine is a bit green in this manifestation but generous with typical peachy-citrus-white-nut flavours; 12% alcohol.

WHITE WINES

NEW ZEALAND

🍷 8 **Freeman's Bay Pinot Gris 2018** £5.99
The sort of spicy but fresh dry white that makes such good drinking with Asian dishes – stands up to assertive flavours and delivers flavours of its own; self-evidently well-made; 13% alcohol.

🍷 8 **Freeman's Bay Sauvignon Blanc 2018** £5.99
Inviting asparagus and seagrass whiff from this consistent Marlborough perennial leads into convincing matching fruit; 12.5% alcohol. A better buy than the heftier but pricier Exquisite Collection Kiwi Sauvignon.

PORTUGAL

🍷 8 **The Wine Foundry Avesso 2018** £6.49
It's a vinho verde, but from some grape called the Avesso (vv's made with other varieties), with green but not spritzy and meadow fresh fruit; 12.5%. Much more likeable than Aldi's admittedly cheaper but distinctly dull Animus Vinho Verde.

SPAIN

🍷 8 **Toro Loco Blanco 2018** £4.69
Attractive floral nose on this tangy and rather slight dry party white from Utiel-Requena; 11.5% alcohol.

🍷 8 **Baron Amarillo Rioja Blanco 2018** £5.99
Modern unoaked dry style but with a good measure of the sunny lushness of the constituent Viura grape; 13% alcohol.

🍷 9 **Exquisite Collection Rias Baixas Albariño 2018** £6.49
Heroically assertive brassica-and-brine seagrass fresh and generously orchard-fruity Atlantic shore dry white of arresting character for every kind of fishy dishy and just about everything else; 12% alcohol.

SPARKLING WINES

FRANCE

♃ 9 **Crémant de Loire Blanc de Noir** £7.99
Very dry but brightly flavoursome 'creaming' sparkler
from black Cabernet Franc grapes – more familiar in the
region's bracingly delicious red wines – this is orchard-
fruit fresh with background redcurrant notes; 12%
alcohol. Thrillingly good.

♃ 9 **Crémant du Jura 2016** £8.29
Pure Chardonnay fizz from hill country east of Burgundy
is remarkably lush with crisp-apple fruit and freshly
appealing; 13% alcohol. Consistent perennial favourite.

♃ 8 **Veuve Monsigny Champagne Brut** £12.49
Aldi house champagne has moved up in price from last
year's £10.99 but still impresses for value: inviting bakery
aroma, lively mousse and crisp white fruits; 12% alcohol.

♃ 8 **Veuve Monsigny Champagne Brut**
Grand Reserve £14.99
Presumably longer-bottle-aged than the basic brut this
does have noticeably more heft and mellowness and
might very well develop with a year or two's keeping;
12.5% alcohol.

♃ 8 **Philizot Champagne Brut 2014** £19.99
An Aldi exclusive sold only online this young single-
vintage all-Chardonnay certainly impressed: proper
brioche whiff, stirringly de luxe fruit in the creamy
mousse; 12.5% alcohol. Should evolve for years.

ITALY

♃ 8 **Collezione Oro Low Sugar Prosecco** £8.99
An interesting novelty bobbing about in the lake that is
prosecco. A dieter's fizz that tastes naturally wholesome
as well as unsweetened; 11% alcohol.

Asda

Whither Asda? Now that the proposed blending with Sainsbury's has withered on the vine and US owner WalMart is rumoured to be seeking a disposal, the future looks uncertain. How this relates to the day-to-day fortunes of the business looks equally unclear but from my narrow viewpoint, the corporate confusion isn't doing Asda any favours. The wine range is diminished and the extreme variation in choice between the branches is no longer redeemed by the online Wine Shop service, which shut down in 2018.

All that said, there are still good wines. Nothing much new, but maybe that can be attributed to temporary stasis arising from the Sainsbury's saga. Prices are still keen – Asda is unquestionably the most competitive with Aldi and Lidl – and there are old favourites on good form from the outstanding 2018 vintage in Europe.

House champagne under the Louis Bernard label is terrific, and I am relieved that the best true Lambrusco on the market, Solato, is still there. Among a crowd of good dry whites from Italy, the Falanghina Beneventano from the Campania is a standout.

Finally, a revelation. I had long assumed that the name Asda is a simple contraction of Associated Dairies, begetter of the chain. Well, it isn't. It's an elision of Asquith and Dairies. Asquith brothers Peter and Fred, butchers and grocers from West Yorkshire, merged their outlets with Associated's stores in 1965 and thus Asda. So now you know.

RED WINES

ARGENTINA

🍷 8 **Extra Special
Malbec 2018** £7.50
It has the expected charred savour to the dark fruit, but
nicely aligned with sweet berry ripeness in an easy, well-
judged weight; 13.5% alcohol.

AUSTRALIA

🍷 8 **Extra Special Yarra Valley Pinot
Noir 2018** £9.00
Typical pale Pinot colour gives way to equally typical
robust Aussie Pinot style, generous in lingering cherry-
raspberry heft complete with clingy dry finish; 13%
alcohol.

CHILE

🍷 9 **Winemaker's Choice Pinot Noir 2018** £4.25
Amazingly cheap but emphatically expressive earthy
Pinot in the fully ripened Chilean style; there is 15%
Syrah in the mix, and why not? Substantial summer red;
12.5% alcohol.

🍷 8 **Extra Special Carmenère 2017** £6.50
Rich dark colour, concentrated cassis nose and layered
black-cherry-chocolate-plum flavours; fun food red
(steak and chips) from Colchagua Valley; 13.5% alcohol.

FRANCE

🍷 8 **Costières de Nîmes Cuvée Réserve 2017** £7.00
Recognisable fruits-of-the-forest ruggedly abrading style
to this artfully fashioned intense spicy Midi red; winter
warmer for meaty menus; 14% alcohol.

🍷 8 **Winemaker's Choice Claret 2018** £7.00
You could argue that the antediluvian branding bodes ill
but it's a fine modern wine, plump with Merlot fruit from
what has evidently been an auspicious vintage, bright and
new but already drinking well; 13.5% alcohol.

RED WINES

FRANCE

**7 Plan de Dieu Côtes du Rhône
Villages 2018**   **£9.00**
Beetroot-coloured with a dark heart of liquorice spiciness
this is a substantial wine (14% alcohol) still tasting a bit
hard in summer 2019 and maybe in need of time to come
round. Might just be from overripe fruit, given the 2018
heat in the Rhône.

ITALY

10 Solato Lambrusco   **£6.50**
Deep purple colour, violet and blackberry nose and a shy
but noticeable effervescence to convey the joyful bright
berry fruits of this wholly authentic Emilia-Romagna
non-vintage wine. It's the best imaginable picnic red,
fresh and dry-finishing and must be enjoyed thoroughly
chilled; 11% alcohol. And it's £1 cheaper than last year.

8 Villa Vincini Gran Rosso 2018   **£7.50**
It's six parts Merlot and four Corvina, the grape of
Valpolicella, combining into a deep purple, charmingly
plump cherry fruit with a good taut acidity in the
approved Italian manner; wholesome and balanced from
the Veneto; 14% alcohol.

8 Villa Vincini Governo 2016   **£9.50**
Dark Tuscan wine made with the addition of sun-dried
grapes (*governo*) has a sinful sweet toffee nose but the
fruit is artfully raspy and brisk with plummy Chianti-
style cherry fruits and a proper nutskin-dry finish; 13.5%
alcohol. Nice contrivance for pasta nights.

PORTUGAL

8 Extra Special Douro 2017   **£6.00**
Perennial favourite from the Port country is appropriately
dark, spicy and intense with a good grip of tannin and a
lot of dark savour, all at an unusually modest price for
table wine from this region; 13.5% alcohol.

RED WINES

PORTUGAL

🍷 8 **Bodacious 2017** £8.00

Oxford dictionaries dismiss the word as American 20th-century slang, a portmanteau of bold and audacious; whatever, it seems a foolhardy description for a wine from the Alentejo but don't be put off. A mix of Cabernet Sauvignon with indigenous Aragonez and Castelão, it has hearty juicy plummy dark fruit with traditional Portuguese clove, cinnamon and mint traces; 13.5% alcohol.

SPAIN

🍷 8 **Extra Special Marques del Norte**
Reserva Rioja 2015 £8.00

Intense opaque colour prepares you for this still-youthful reserva wine abounding in vigorous fruit and vanilla creaminess with a firm grip of tannin to wrap it all up; it will surely continue to evolve in the bottle, as these wines are intended to do; 14% alcohol.

PINK WINES

FRANCE

🍷 8 **Le Cellier de Saint Louis Provence**
Rosé 2017 £8.00

Varois wine has attractive pale copper colour, cheerful floral aroma and a crisp array of pink flavours finishing very dry and brisk; 13% alcohol.

🍷 8 **Luminière Rosé 2018** £9.00

Pale salmon colour, elegant spare cool pink fruit with citrus highlights, nicely made Provence dry wine tastes special; 13% alcohol.

ITALY

🍷 8 **Negroamaro Rosé 2018** £7.50

Puglian dry wine veers near to magenta in colour and delivers matchingly ripe (well, veering to sweet) red-fruit flavours; 12% alcohol. A food wine, I'd say.

WHITE WINES

8 **Norton Libre Torrontes 2018** £7.50

Torrontes is Argentina's own indigenous variety, mostly making unremarkable grapy off-dry whites. This is untypically dry, bright and interesting; 13% alcohol.

8 **DOT Chardonnay 2018** £8.00

DOT stands for Diversity of Terroirs, meaning I suppose that the wine is a blend of Chardonnay grapes trucked in from here there and everywhere in the region of origin, Mendoza in the Andean foothills. This is a common practice; might as well make a virtue of it. Nice straight apple-crisp example; 13% alcohol.

8 **Norton Barrel Select Chardonnay 2018** £8.50

Familiar Mendoza brand has a bit of brassica lift as well as peachy oaked fresh fruit, dry but plenty of ripeness; 13.5% alcohol.

8 **Extra Special Barossa Valley Chardonnay 2018** £7.00

Safe bet. Part of it is reportedly barrel-fermented and you get the concomitant coconutty creaminess amid the fresh flow of sweet-apple fruit; nifty balance and dry as you like; 13.5% alcohol.

9 **Côtes du Rhône Blanc 2017** £7.00

Immediately likeable dry blend at a keen price; tastes lush and fresh, peachy and peary, tangy and fleetingly rich. I am reminded that white Châteauneuf du Pape no better than this goes for more than twice the price; 13.5% alcohol.

WHITE WINES

FRANCE

9 Limoux 2017   £7.00

Languedoc Chardonnay is jiggling with ripe natural-tasting sweet-apple lush fruit in endearingly healthy balance with long, slaking flavours and freshness; a very pleasant surprise; 13% alcohol.

8 Languedoc Blanc 2018   £7.00

Interesting grape blend – Grenache (Blanc), Marsanne and Bourboulenc – makes for a nuanced basket of white and exotic fruit flavours coming out dry and fresh; 12.5% alcohol.

9 Saint-Chinian Blanc 2018   £8.00

You don't see much of this, at least not in UK supermarkets. St Chinian is a rugged hill-country Languedoc backwater known for characterful reds that has only had an AC for whites since 2004 and here's a good one with a nectarine balance of ripeness and twang, very fresh and intriguing, finishing long and very trim; 13% alcohol.

8 Extra Special Pouilly Fumé 2018   £12.00

Very proper example of this renowned Loire Valley Sauvignon, pebbly fresh and emphatically grassy and lush; I preferred it to Asda's Sancerre by a long chalk; 13% alcohol.

GERMANY

8 Winemaker's Choice Riesling 2018   £4.75

From the Rheinpfalz, it's softly sweet but with a trace of Riesling raciness and a lift of acidity; 11% alcohol.

WHITE WINES

8 **Farmers of Wine Organic White** £5.50
Worthy-sounding non-vintage party bottle is wrapped
cryptically in brown paper but turns out well enough with
floral pong, fruit salad flavours, even a little blanched
almond richness and a crisp edge; 12.5% alcohol.

9 **Diverso Falanghina Beneventano 2017** £7.50
Prickly fresh on the nose and greengage-grassy-grapefruit
alliterative attractions in the crisp white fruit (pineapple
too as an afterthought) this Campania wine stands out
in spite of the current fashionableness of the Falanghina
grape; 12.5% alcohol.

8 **Lugana 2018** £8.50
Popular Lake Garda (Veneto) dry white delivers a lot of
peach and apple lush/crisp fruit in elegant balance and
finishes very brisk; 13% alcohol.

8 **Cascina Valentino Roero Arneis 2018** £9.50
Recherché Piedmont dry wine has an artful balance of
ripeness (13.5% alcohol) and heft with grassy-lemony
tang and long, lasting orchard-fruit flavours; it tastes as
expensive as it is and makes an impression.

8 **Extra Special Rueda**
Verdejo 2018 £6.00
Sharpish very crisp and lemony pure varietal from
creditable Castille DO is fun and good value; 13% alcohol.

WHITE WINES

SPAIN

🍷 8 **Extra Special Albariño 2018**   £8.00
Good hit of crisp seaside-fresh fruit from this broad-flavoured Rias Baixas wine, authentically expressive of its Atlantic-facing locality; plenty of interest and a good partner for fish and shellfish of all descriptions; 13% alcohol.

SPARKLING WINES

ENGLAND

🍷 8 **Extra Special English Sparkling**   £21.00
Surrey plantings of the Champagne varieties Pinot Noir, Chardonnay and Pinot Meunier make this well-coloured vintage (2015) and vividly fruity and fresh fizz into something quite closely resembling the model over the Channel; 12% alcohol. Note that the price is the same as Asda's own Premier Cru Champagne.

🍷 9 **Extra Special Crémant de Loire**   £9.00
Proper creamy mousse and fleeting honey aroma from the 80% Chenin Blanc in this blend (the rest is Chardonnay and Pinot Noir) make this such an appealing sparkler, full of fun and freshness at a very friendly price; 12% alcohol.

FRANCE

🍷 9 **Extra Special Champagne Premier Cru Brut**   £21.00
Under the Louis Bernard brand, this really is quite special; beckoning bakery smell, mellow fruit full of orchard zest and trim gently citrus crispness; not as I remember it in previous years – better; 12.5% alcohol.

SPARKLING WINES

ITALY

🍷 7 **Alberto Nani Organic Prosecco** £9.00
I dutifully tasted my way round the proseccos, and chose
this one for its eager froth, decently crisp pear fruit, and
'brut' style dryness; 11% alcohol.

——*The Co-operative*——

The Co-op is going from strength to strength. The annual tastings are a revelation to me as I don't otherwise get to try many of the wines from my local stores. I took this up with wine buyer Ben Cahill. Yes, he quite understood. While splendid Château Vieux Manoir appears in 2,468 shops, glorious Reichsgraf von Kesselstatt Riesling figures in only 201.

Many of the best Co-op wines are made in modest quantity, but help is at hand in seeking them out. 'Haven't you heard about the Co-op Wine Locator?' Ben asks me. It's an online service. You go to the Co-op home page, click on Co-op Food and then on Wines. There's a Find a Wine search box. Type in the name of the wine, go to the 'find this product' box, put your postcode in and get a list of the nearest branches stocking it.

It's so straightforward that even a computer nincompoop like me can operate it.

This year seek out a run of excellent Malbecs from Argentina including Fairtrade brands and new red wine Biferno from Molise in southern Italy. I urge you to try it – from any one of 463 stores or, of course, with the aid of the Locator.

From Sicily, Vanita Grillo is one of the most thrilling dry whites of the year, and Balfour 1503 Foxwood Cuvee, a sparkler from Tonbridge in Kent is the first English wine I have to date given a top score. It is preternaturally good.

RED WINES

8 Co-op Fairtrade Bonarda-Malbec 2018 £5.25

There's an Italian savour to this 70/30 blend, adding bright cherry plumpness to the customary Malbec toasty meatiness; friendly weight, 13% alcohol and keen price.

10 Hereford Tempranillo 2018 £7.00

Beefy branding of Argentine wines usually denotes Malbec, but this is all Tempranillo, better known as the backbone of Spain's Rioja, and in this vintage it has made an outstandingly complete, natural-tasting cassis-plum unoaked and ideally weighted red wine of character; 13% alcohol. Brilliant.

9 Co-op Fairtrade Irresistible Malbec 2017 £7.50

Inky maroon colour, sweet blackberry pong and dark fruit flavours smoothed with oak contact but lucid and complete, this is special as well as worthy (from famed Famatima Fairtrade enterprise La Riojana) in a very attractive package; 13% alcohol.

10 Vinalba Finca La 70 Malbec Cabernet Sauvignon 2017 £9.00

Wild maroon colour is matched by the exuberant briar-sweet, blueberry-bramble fruits, a proper blast of joyful flavours that linger long and trim up with ideal acidity; all told, a piece of Patagonian perfection; 14.5% alcohol.

9 The Unexpected Red 2018 £6.75

I assume only adventurous shoppers are prepared to take a punt on this, so for the more cautious customer please be assured it's a pleasant surprise. It's four parts Cabernet Sauvignon, three Sagrantino (big inky reds in Umbria, Italy) and three Merlot/Tempranillo, giving dense beetroot colour, big clingy black-fruit flavours and Italian-style nutskin-dry finish; 13.5% alcohol and good value.

ARGENTINA

AUSTRALIA

RED WINES

AUSTRALIA

🍷 8 **The Interlude Pinot Noir 2018** £7.00
Bright garnet colour and an alluring purity of flavour mark out this discreetly oaked raspberry-cherry-scented middleweight; impressive in its own way – nicely controlled ripeness; 13.5% alcohol.

CHILE

🍷 8 **Sentador Cabernet Sauvignon 2018** £6.00
Lively young-tasting but boldly fruity marginally oaky proper varietal (actually it has 10% Syrah in the mix) is rich in crimson colour and plumply ripe; 13% alcohol.

FRANCE

🍷 9 **Château Vieux Manoir 2017** £6.75
Universal (stocked in 2,468 Co-op stores) perennial claret on particularly good form in this vintage is healthily ripe and developed, the blackcurrant fruit lively and unoaked but comfortingly rounded; 13.5% alcohol. Good value.

🍷 8 **Côtes du Rhône La Grange St Martin 2016** £7.75
Good dark wine from a maturing vintage with likeable spicy abrasion – ideal match for starchy rustic delights like cassoulet; 13.5% alcohol.

🍷 8 **Château Capitoul 2017** £8.00
Deeply maroon Languedoc winter wine has toasty spicy black-fruit ripeness and an impressive integrity of flavour with a gentle grip of tannin; 13% alcohol.

RED WINES

FRANCE

🍷 10 Domaine des Ormes Saumur 2016 £8.00

I am a veritable propagandist for the vigorous red wines of the Loire made from Cabernet Franc to convey unique flavours of leafy, even stalky, red fruits with freshness and abrasion. But the few appellations concerned, such as Bourgueil, Chinon and this one, Saumur, are scant in the supermarkets. Here's an out-and-out classic: purple hue, bright blueberry aroma, crunchy-leafy juicy flavours and aboundingly ripe, even round, in its exuberant fruit; 12.5% alcohol.

🍷 7 Les Cardinaux 2016 £10.00

'The Cardinals' is presumably a nod to the Châteauneuf du Pape connections of the Perrin family (they own esteemed Château Beaucastel), makers of this expensive Côtes du Rhône. It's OK but a bit tough and might well develop into something good in time. There's a clue on the back label: 'A real vin de garde' it says; 13% alcohol.

🍷 9 Domaine Les Grandes Costes Pic-Saint-Loup 2016 £15.25

Top-drawer wine from a newly elevated Languedoc appellation has opaque deep colour and gorgeous plush silky Syrah fruit abounding with spicy nuance; drinking very well already, it will surely evolve for years; 14.5% alcohol.

🍷 9 Château Beau-Site 2014 £22.00

Renowned cru bourgeois claret from the St Estèphe commune of the Médoc in a pretty good vintage is well up to the mark – and even to the price. It's impressively dense in colour and savour, luxuriously perfumed and hefty with cassis fruit and the traditional grand Bordeaux suggestions of violet, cigar box (if you can remember that cedary old relic of yesteryear) and liquorice (pontefract cake to be more precise); robust but approachable now, it will develop for many years yet; 13% alcohol.

RED WINES

ITALY

🍷 **10** **Molise Biferno Riserva 2014** £8.00

I've been following this obscure southern Italian oddity for years but have never before found it in a supermarket. Bravo for the Co-op! It's a woody old thing, deeply succulent, curiously sweet, pruny and minty and off-the-wall, but I find it irresistible and must award maximum points, if only for diversity; 13% alcohol.

🍷 **9** **Casa Nardelli Cuvee Carolina 2017** £9.00

It's a kind of Supertuscan, made by venerable Chianti estate Castello Vicchiomaggio from nine parts Sangiovese to one of Cabernet Sauvignon and it's silkily, spicily and seductively delicious, much in the riserva (oaked) Chianti style finishing taut and brisk; 13.5% alcohol.

PORTUGAL

🍷 **9** **Rabelo 2015** £6.00

On the shelf at my tiny local Co-op this caught my eye. It had a protruding cork you can pull by hand. I guess it's a pioneer, Portugal being the home of the cork as well as the Rabelo, a Douro river boat for wine casks. Thus this wine made at the Adega Vila Real in the heart of Port country, soft, plump with elderberry-bramble fruit harvested years back and making a most friendly and warming bargain red at 13% alcohol.

SPAIN

🍷 **9** **Co-op Old Vine Garnacha 2018** £5.35

Raw-looking but easy-going vigorous brambly Campo de Borja bargain is complete and balanced; 14% alcohol. Well contrived.

RED WINES

8 **Rioja Gran Familia** £6.00

Mass-production generic wine (my bottle was numbered 864236) is cheap, non-vintage and untypical of Rioja, but juicy and balanced; 13% alcohol. Ignore the back-label claim that it 'will improve in your cellar for up to three years' and enjoy now, while it lasts.

8 **Davida 2018** £8.00

Muscular but sweetly savoury dark horse from Navarra (overshadowed neighbour to Rioja) has black sinewy fruit and good grip; 14% alcohol. It's a low-sulphur wine but tastes fine.

8 **El Viejo de Ramon Bilbao Rioja**
Reserva 2014 50cl £8.00

Vigorous darkly ripe smoothie in an interesting bottle size is all Garnacha – no Tempranillo – but definitely reserva Rioja in style; 13.5% alcohol.

8 **Domador Rioja Reserva 2014** £10.00

Fine ruby colour looks pale and the fruit is delicate but I did like the creamily silky cassis-fruit style; 13% alcohol. Drink now, it's not for keeping.

PINK WINES

8 **Incarnade Pinot Noir Rosé 2018** £7.00

Discreet shell-pink colour to this politely fruity and fresh Languedoc pure Pinot Noir is echoed in the delicate strawberry savour, finishing crisp and very dry; 11.5% alcohol.

SPAIN

FRANCE

PINK WINES

8 **La Vieille Ferme Rosé 2018** £7.75
Appetising pale tawny-pink colour, fleeting strawberry
scent, fresh red-fruit style in neat citrus trim, an attractive
brand by Rhône dynasty Famille Perrin; 12.5% alcohol.

8 **Studio by Miraval 2018** £12.00
This jolly nice, crisp 13% alcohol pale dry rosé in a chi-
chi bottle is from starry Provence estate Château Miraval
(props Brad Pitt and Angelina Jolie) and signposts the
recording studio established there by previous owner
Jacques Loussier, maestro of Bach keyboard music, who
by chance died aged 84 in March 2019, just as this wine
was being launched.

8 **Somos Cantina 34 Dry Rosé 2018** £5.50
Party-frock pink from Valencia features a formidably naff
party-themed label bearing the slogan 'Dry Rosé' which it
isn't, but I couldn't help liking the cheerful, floral style –
and the price; 11.5% alcohol.

WHITE WINES

9 **Finca Las Moras Pinot Grigio
Trebbiano 2018** £7.25
Odd-seeming 50/50 mixture of Italian grapes triumphs
in this delightfully crisp apple-and-pear refresher from
the high-altitude, super-sunny San Juan region; there's an
Italian-style blanched-almond creaminess and a twang of
lemon, too; 13% alcohol.

WHITE WINES

AUSTRALIA

🍷 8 **Barton Vineyard Vermentino 2018** £8.25
Vermentino is said to be the coming thing in Italian white wine, after first coming to light in Sardinia. Here's a variation on the theme from Riverland in South Australia, very pale but briskly fresh and lemony – and even just a little Italian in style; 12% alcohol.

🍷 9 **Laneway Chardonnay 2017** £9.00
From the state of Victoria, it's positively succulent, as rich in peaches-and-cream oaked Chardonnay ripeness as it is in colour but poised and mineral in its nature; 12.5% alcohol. Aussie chardy for grown-ups.

AUSTRIA

🍷 9 **Eitzinger Grüner Veltliner 2017** £8.75
Grown in the well-rated Kamptal region, Austria's indigenous grape comes out in rich colour, white-pepper aromas and ripe, sweet-apple flavours, fresh but exotic and all in alluring balance; fascinating aperitif and a nifty match for fish or fowl; 12.5% alcohol.

CHILE

🍷 8 **Yali Wild Swan Sauvignon Blanc 2018** £7.50
Compared to New Zealand or France's Loire Valley, Chile can struggle a bit for identity in the Sauvignon Blanc stakes, but this blandly presented brand puts in a good effort. It has that special ripeness that Chile can do, but has a brassica acidity all its own too; generous, easy-drinking, endearing; 12.5% alcohol.

WHITE WINES

8 La Vieille Ferme Blanc 2018 £7.75
Safe Rhône brand with reassuring chickens on the label
has regionally typical free-ranging flavours incorporating
peach and pear, even pineapple, all happily counterpointed
by citrussy tang; 13% alcohol.

9 Co-op Irresistible Marsanne 2018 £8.00
Standout Pays d'Oc dry white by busy Jean-Claude Mas
intrigues immediately with its apple-blossom and brassica
scents, warmly sunny lingering stone-fruit flavours and
suggestion of vanilla richness (some new oak cask ageing
here) and smart balance; 13% alcohol.

8 Wolfberger Gewürztraminer 2016 £9.25
From the oldest wine co-op in Alsace, a pleasingly hefty
Gewürz with gold colour, lychee perfume and long spicy-
smoky flavours; the sweetness is controlled and healthy;
13% alcohol.

9 Co-op Irresistible Chablis 2018 £12.50
Fine flinty-ripe classic wine by Chablis leading light Jean-
Marc Brocard is the first finished product I tasted from
the big and beautiful 2018 harvest across Burgundy – and
it certainly augurs well for Chablis; lovely balanced wine
full of mineral Chardonnay life and twangy with citrus
zing; 12.5% alcohol.

WHITE WINES

8 **Kleine Kapelle Pinot Grigio 2018** £6.00

Simple grapy Rheinpfalz dry wine is smoky, slaty-fresh and a welcome variation on the Italian theme; 12% alcohol.

10 **Reichsgraf von Kesselstatt Riesling Spätlese 2016** £12.00

I thought this was the next vintage of last year's Riesling Trocken 2015 from Von Kesslestatt but it is instead a return to the QmP wine from the famed Mosel estate's Goldtröpfchen vineyards, as featured by the Co-op for many years past, this time for a fabulously good *spätlese* wine. It's perfect: honeyed aroma of startling richness gives way to luscious apple fruit racing with minerally freshness and exuberance, beautifully balanced and just 9% alcohol.

8 **Verdicchio dei Castelli di Jesi 2018** £6.00

The town of Jesi in Ancona, a province of Italy's Marches, stands at the centre of a great number of little villages, each clustered round a castle – thus the location name of this wine, once renowned as the 'white Barolo'. This everyday dry wine has no such pretensions. It has a little of the green lustre of the grander wines but rather a lot of residual sugar; fun, though, and an amazingly irrelevant Venusian label; 12.5% alcohol.

10 **Vanita Grillo 2018** £7.00

From sequestered Sambuca di Sicilia, in the news in 2019 for offering homes for sale at one euro in a bid to counter depopulation, a crunchy-orchard-fruit charmer of preternatural freshness, with underlying mango-nectarine flavours balanced by tangy grapefruit and lemon; 12% alcohol. Star wine with a baroque label from local grape variety Grillo.

WHITE WINES

NEW ZEALAND

8 Co-op Runestone Sauvignon Blanc 2018   £7.00
Grassy-nettly Marlborough wine has a bit of Chardonnay
in the mix and I reckon it shows – trace of sweet apple
amid the gooseberries; 12% alcohol.

8 Peter Yealands Sauvignon Blanc 2018   £9.50
Snappy Sauvignon fruit, crisply green in its expansive
grassiness in this keen wine from a much-admired
Marlborough producer; 12.5% alcohol. Safe bet.

PORTUGAL

7 Escudo Real Vinho Verde 2018   £6.00
Novelty wine has prickly zip to the white fruit but turns
out quite sweet – which is presumably what the market
for vinho verde expects; 9.5% alcohol. At least it's cheap.

SPAIN

8 Cune Rioja Blanco 2017   £9.50
Barrel-fermented but by no means old-fashioned white
Rioja has creaminess as well as fresh, lemony fruit
flavours, all nicely balanced; 13% alcohol.

FORTIFIED

PORTUGAL

8 Sandeman White Port   £10.00
New from Sandeman (to me anyway) a mellow rather
than sweet port of gold colour and rich, ardent flavours;
it's intended as an aperitif and is best enjoyed thoroughly
chilled; 19.5% alcohol.

SPARKLING WINES

ENGLAND

10 Balfour 1503 Foxwood Cuvee £17.50

Hush Heath near Tonbridge in Kent is an old estate complete with spectacular timbered manor house built in 1503, vineyards first planted in 2002 and now a new winery and visitor centre. I've followed the wines and often liked them, and now this: a bang-on English Sparkling Wine of lovable character at a realistic price. From the champagne-grape varieties Chardonnay and Pinots Noir and Meunier, it is 'brut' (dry) in style, has pale gold colour, farmhouse-loaf aroma, mellow ripe fruit urged along in the fine-bubble persisting mousse; 11.5% alcohol. Yes, it's a match even for good champagne. My flag-waving fizz of the year, and apparently exclusive to the Co-op.

FRANCE

9 Les Pionniers Champagne Brut £18.99

Consistently likeable house champagne made by Piper Heidsieck and commemorating the Rochdale Pioneers who founded the first modern co-operative movement in 1844. Nice suggestion of lemon meringue pie on the nose, fine ripe white fruits in a convincing tiny-bubble rush, fresh and stimulating; 12% alcohol.

Lidl

Another abbreviated entry for Lidl this year, I'm afraid. It's not for the absence of good wine buys at the popular discounter. It's that the best wines are almost invariably among the seasonal ranges put on sale several times a year, selling out in a matter of weeks. I am grateful to Lidl for continuing to invite me to taste the items featured in these 'Wine Tours' but for the purposes of this annual guide, the wines' ephemeral nature consigns them to irrelevance.

All that remains is the 'core range' of consistently stocked wines. They are a rum lot. The few about which I have anything to say appear in the couple of pages that follow this. I have bought them at my local store. Most do not appear here because I can't recommend them, at any price.

RED WINES

ITALY

8 Barolo 2014   **£11.99**
Mentioned in this space last year, this vintage was still on shelf as I went to press in autumn 2019. I haven't retasted it and the price has moved up from £9.99 (maybe that's why it's stuck) but it's a fair bet it will be coming along nicely, the limpid cherry-berry fruit rounding out into silkiness and complexity; 14% alcohol.

PORTUGAL

8 Azinhaga de Ouro Douro Reserva 2016   **£5.99**
Inky table wine from Port country is certainly indicative of the style of the great fortified wine with spice and hefty ripeness to the fore, but it's not overdone and delivers bright blackcurrant fruits with a gentle creaminess from barrel contact; 13.5% alcohol.

SOUTH AFRICA

8 Cimarosa South Africa Pinotage 2016   **£3.89**
Impressively consistent indigenous varietal at a consistently impressive price. You get the characteristic tarry savour of the grape but not at the expense of lively juiciness; 14% alcohol.

RED WINES

SPAIN

8 Baturrica Gran Reserva 2011   £4.99
Baked blackcurrant fruit is to the fore in this long-aged
Tarragona monster with a suggestion of mulberry in the
grippy dark fruit; it's really quite something for this kind
of money and smartly packaged, complete with old-
fashioned Spanish-style wire cage; 13% alcohol.

8 Cepa Lebrel Rioja Reserva 2013   £5.79
This must be the cheapest Rioja Reserva on the market,
and I like it better than some lately tasted at higher prices.
It's light in style but sleek with creamy blackcurrant
juiciness and wearing its age well; 13.5% alcohol.

9 Priorat Crianza Vinya Carles 2014   £6.99
In last year's edition I included this Catalan wine (same
vintage) on the proviso it was not from the core range
and might have disappeared. Well it's still very much on
shelf, up in price from £5.99 but otherwise as before:
discreetly oaked medium-heft, sweet-violet-perfumed ripe
blackberry flavours in good balance; 14% alcohol.

WHITE WINES

CHILE

8 Cimarosa Pedro Jimenez 2018   £4.29
The Pedro Jimenez might be more familiar as the
sweetening grape in sherry, or even, in Chile, as the source
for the fierce brandy known as Pisco, but in this aromatic
wine it's a pleasantly refreshing citrus-edged dry white at
12% alcohol and a bargain price.

WHITE WINES

GERMANY

🍷 8 Brauneberger Kurfürstlay Mosel Riesling 2017 £4.99

Fresh peach-and-apple moselle of racy flavour and delicate balance, grapy rather than sweet and 10.5% alcohol. Given the retailer's nationality, can't we be offered more from Germany?

SPAIN

🍷 8 Cepa Lebrel Rioja Blanco 2018 £4.99

Bit of colour and sweet orchard-fruit aroma to this plump white Rioja with hints of preserved fruits and maybe even creaminess but dry in style and not without freshness; 12.5% alcohol.

🍷 8 Abellio Albariño Rias Baixas 2017 £5.99

Easy-drinking popular style from Atlantic-facing vineyards has suitably fresh and breezy seagrass white fruits and plenty of ripeness; 12.5% alcohol.

FORTIFIED

PORTUGAL

🍷 8 Armilar 10-Year-Old Tawny Port £10.99

Gaudy bottling by C da Silva has proper copper colour of long-wood-aged port and an eager figgy-nutty-rosehip nose; it's light in weight but with plenty of sweet fruit and fire for the modest price; 20% alcohol. Winter seasonal.

Marks & Spencer

To date, it has vaguely nagged me that M&S isn't really a supermarket. Now, all doubt is banished. In 2019 the retailer announced plans to open food stores laid out and sized just like supermarkets. What's more, M&S products will become available on Ocado ('the online supermarket') in 2020, in place of Waitrose's.

As a key part of this new strategy, M&S has cut the prices of more than 1,000 products, including wines. Drinks boss Rebecca Adams says they are 'significantly cutting back the prices on some of our most popular wines, offering some of the best value on the high street'.

You get the drift. And she adds: 'The best news is that none of this work has impacted the quality of our wines; we haven't changed a drop or a blend to save money'.

It's true. The wines are as consistently inspired as ever, and in many cases noticeably cheaper. Highlights include a new range of Riojas, with the crianza standing out particularly, and my favourite Soave of the year, which happens to be among the wines at a reduced price. Australian whites are on great form, including a new generic blend priced at just a fiver.

The M&S wine website, offering six-bottle cases with free delivery on orders above £100 continues but the range has been reduced in number. You'll find all the wines on promo highlighted, but I fear the 25%-off deals for multibuys may now appear less often.

RED WINES

ARGENTINA

🍷 8 Butcher's Block Shiraz Bonarda 2018 £6.00
Some of the grapes in this were 'thermo-vinified' to intensify the flavours and I reckon it shows. There's a roastiness to the fruit that might suggest overripeness but does lend a wholesome almost raisiny savour; distinctive balanced wine with a modest 12.5% alcohol.

🍷 8 El Cuando Merlot 2018 £7.00
Well-defined Merlot has the expected sweetly juicy plumpness and a pleasantly surprising briskness of acidity that gives it appealing balance; 12.5% alcohol. Nicely contrived.

AUSTRALIA

🍷 8 Australian Red £5.00
Non-vintage bargain blend has alluring ruby colour, bright blackberry aromas and a sneaky creaminess trimmed to a dry, clean edge; 13% alcohol. Good party red for this money.

🍷 8 Pichi Richi Shiraz 2018 £6.00
Plausible soft mellow fruit is lifted by bright acidity; plumptious but not overripe, it grows on you; 14% alcohol.

🍷 9 Burra Brook Cabernet Sauvignon 2018 £7.00
Old school Aussie Cab, I've scribbled in my note, 'like souped-up claret'. Which might be a bit unfair, because this isn't just the extra-ripened blackcurrant style of yesteryear Down Under, it's the M&S extra-ripened … (well, you know the rest). This is a perennial favourite on fine form, big in fruit, yes, but balanced, wholesome and 14% alcohol.

RED WINES

8 Barossa Merlot 2017 £8.00

There's more Merlot at M&S than I remember before and this one's a welcome find at a New Lower Price. Pitch dark in colour, the fruit corresponds with proper Merlot deep sweet choc'n'cherry savour nicely tidied up with firm tannins; 14.5% alcohol.

9 Côtes du Rhône 2016 £6.00

From the best vintage for years in the southern Rhône this nicely rounded wine has a fine pale garnet colour, vivid spicy red-fruit nose and wholesome matching fruit with 13.5% alcohol. It is also jolly cheap. What's not to like?

8 Duc de Chaleray 2017 £6.00

Who would guess what this M&S new addition is? Turns out it's a Languedoc lightweight from mainly Carignan, mixed with Merlot and Grenache, delivering juicy, just-squished red-fruit flavours in gleeful abundance with a Beaujolais-like weight and neat, clean balance; 12% alcohol.

8 Le Froglet Shiraz 2018 £7.00

Brand names like this make me hopping mad and I croak at the craven use by French producers of Australia's 'Shiraz' for indigenous Syrah, but I did like this Languedoc confection for its youthful purple pizzazz, bright briary fruit and lipsmacking tannins; 13.5% alcohol.

6 Beaujolais 2018 £7.00

Down to £7 from the 2017 vintage's £9 this seemed to me still too expensive; it was a bit hard, as if made from overripe fruit, and lacking the expected bouncy charm; 13% alcohol.

RED WINES

8 Domaine Mandeville Pinot Noir 2018 £8.00
An old M&S friend at a New Lower Price, it's a Languedoc
burgundy-style red with more colour and substance than
you'd get from most actual burgundy at £8; ample with
mellow cherry Pinot fruit and 13% alcohol.

9 Coteaux Bourguignons 2018 £8.50
Loved the blue tinge in the colour of this vivid pure
Gamay, translating into a thrillingly juicy and crunchy
young Beaujolais-Burgundy mash-up alive with red-
summer-fruit lushness; 13% alcohol. Fine aperitif to
drink cool, or with white meats, charcuterie, even salads.

8 Château Gillet 2017 £8.50
Bordeaux wine from a so-so vintage in the region has
noticeably vivid hedgerow fruit and an immediate
charm; reasonably priced ready-to-drink claret with 13%
alcohol.

9 Château Les Rambauds Malbec 2017 £9.50
Bordeaux red made entirely from the vogueish Malbec (a
vanished blending variety in claret) has the recognisable
warmly ripe thick-skinned plummy style of the grape
complete with a near-caramel richness and spicy darkness
of black fruit; fascinatingly good and a realistic challenge
to Argentine hegemony; 13% alcohol.

8 Fleurie 2018 £10.00
Serious Beaujolais *cru* from what must have been a
seriously sunny ripening season, this was quite sinewy
and tense in its youth (tasted spring 2019), but the
hallmark purple-juicy fruit was abundant and it should
turn out nicely; 13% alcohol.

RED WINES

8 Crozes-Hermitage 2016   £13.50

I've long suspected this relatively humble northern Rhône appellation of trading on the renown of its noble neighbour Hermitage to sell very much less lordly wines at inflated prices. But this one actually isn't too bad with its vigorous, silky, spicy Syrah comfortably abrasive on the palate and coming round to some sort of mature development; 12.5% alcohol.

8 La Fortezza Merlot 2017   £7.00

The Merlot of Bordeaux migrates successfully to Sicily in this thoroughly Italian manifestation by the island's artful Settesoli co-op. Sunnily ripe cherry-blackcurrant juicy fruitiness trimmed up with nutskin-dry acidity to make an ideal sticky-pasta match; 13% alcohol.

8 Valpolicella Valpantena 2018   £7.00

Textbook example of this famous Veronese name has bright and encouragingly intense garnet colour, classic bitter-cherry nose and matching crisp fruit discreetly enriched with blanched-almond creaminess, finishing grippy-dry; 12.5% alcohol.

8 Chianti DOCG 2017   £7.50

Well-defined Chianti embodies the style faithfully with its sweetly ripe cherry fruit in pleasing balance with the acidity, finishing tight and clean; works well at a fair price; 12% alcohol.

9 Nicosia Etna Rosso 2017   £11.00

There's a likeable lemon twang on the nose of this scrummy blueberry-briary-herbaceous wine from the volatile vineyards of Sicily's grumbling volcano; big flavours but mellow silkiness too, very much a wine of its origins; 13% alcohol. Sicily, please note, grows a lot of lemons.

RED WINES

NEW ZEALAND

8 Koha Pinot Noir 2017   £9.00

Limpid garnet colour leads you into an emphatically aromatic pinot evoking cherries-still-on-the-stalks with attractive fresh mouthfeel and neat citrus edge; 12.5% alcohol.

9 Craft 3 Pinot Noir 2017   £13.00

Given that village burgundies like Gevrey-Chambertin now go for £50 a pop, this Kiwi spin on the theme, from Spring Creek, Marlborough, looks cheap. It's a lushly plump raspberry-and-cream Pinot of jewel-like colour and brightness with a good backbone and trademark Kiwi heft, minty and smoky; 12.5% alcohol.

SOUTH AFRICA

8 Star Catcher Shiraz 2018   £7.50

The full name is Star Catcher No Added Sulphur Shiraz 2018, which makes it, I suppose, a 'natural' wine. But you wouldn't guess – it seems perfectly normal to me. Beetroot colour, sweet blackberry nose (definitely no sulphur) and spicy dark fruit; 13.5% alcohol.

**10 Helderberg Winery Cabernet
       Sauvignon 2017**   £9.00

Perfectly contrived pure Cabernet shows thrillingly natural cassis flavours in fine balance with an elegant slinkiness; 14% alcohol. Serious wine from Stellenbosch, which is clearly an ideal habitat, and at a New Lower Price too.

SPAIN

8 Merinas Old Vines Tempranillo 2018   £7.00

From the utterly obscure region of Uclés, south east of Madrid, a big maroon Sunday-roast red with bright blackcurrant savour and wholesome balance; 14% alcohol. The label is decorated with sheep, perhaps Merino.

RED WINES

10 El Duque de Miralta Rioja Crianza 2015   **£10.00**
Level one in M&S's new Rioja range made by El Coto in a top vintage is mellowing in colour and showing sleek vanilla-cassis richness within the clear fruit liveliness; 13.5% alcohol. Delicious soothing wine in prime condition made by M&S's Sue Daniels with 'lovely knowledgeable head winemaker César Fernández' at El Coto.

9 El Duque de Miralta Rioja Reserva 2014   **£12.00**
Sweetly oaked aromas and ample ripeness of well-defined dark, dark blackcurrant fruit set this next one in the new range from El Coto well above the ordinary; very nicely contrived crowd-pleaser; 13.5% alcohol.

8 El Duque de Miralta Rioja Gran
   Reserva 2012   **£15.00**
Dense, soupy rich colour and sweet violet-and-vanilla waft from this still-grippy long-aged deluxe wine, the top tier in the new M&S range; 13.5% alcohol. I was impressed but wondered whether it might not yet need a year or two longer in bottle to reach its silky zenith.

PINK WINES

7 Burra Brook Rosé 2018   **£7.00**
Fruit-salad style without being too syrupy, it has pretty colour and a friendly soft summer red-fruit perfume; 12.5% alcohol.

SPAIN

AUSTRALIA

PINK WINES

9 La Dame en Rose Rosé 2018   £6.00

M&S winemaker Belinda Kleinig is wildly enthusiastic about this new wine from the Midi: 'dry and fruity, a nod to Provence in the colour and taste, and very easy drinking.' Hear hear, say I, wishing to add only that it's a better colour than most wishy-washy Provence pinks and certainly has more fruit flavour, with 11.5% alcohol. It outdoes Provence for value too at £6.00, even competing in the arty-bottle stakes.

8 Gold Label Rosé 2018   £7.00

Old friend from the Languedoc has attractive cerise colour and plenty of fruit interest from a suggestion of rose-hip to crisp redcurrant; dry-finishing and 11.5% alcohol.

8 Sancerre Rosé 2018   £15.00

Very dry almost austere pink wine from the famed Loire appellation is pure Pinot Noir, the skins giving the delicate shade of rosy colour via brief steeping; 13% alcohol. It's elegant and expensive, and it says in my note 'seems to have a Sauvignon-like tang to it'. Well, white Sancerre is all Sauvignon, of course, but the connection can only be by association. If you've got 15 quid, see what you think.

8 House Rosé 2018   £5.00

Salmon-coloured pure Garnacha from the great plain (wine-lake included) of La Mancha has floral and strawberry notes, drinks and finishes really quite fresh and dry and is a modest 11.5% alcohol. Everything you need, really, from a pink wine.

FRANCE

SPAIN

WHITE WINES

9 Australian White £5.00

Not so long ago you'd expect any generic Aussie dry white to be Chardonnay. This one's Colombard with Semillon and a tweak of Viognier; it's a blend of different vintages too, and it's great, generously coloured, vivid with tropical and orchard-white fruits (and redcurrant somewhere), fresh and bright with 12% alcohol. And it is really, really cheap.

8 Pichi Richi Chardonnay 2018 £6.00

Straight dry style is ripe (13.5% alcohol) and peachy, unoaked and honest. Pretty good for the price, and now, I believe, M&S's house Aussie Chardonnay.

9 Barossa Chardonnay 2018 £8.00

Rich lemon-gold colour and a lush peaches and cream aroma lure you into this modern-style (mineral, not woody) dry wine of good heft but poised balance; 12.5% alcohol. M&S's note claims it is 99.9% Chardonnay and 0.1% Sauvignon Blanc, which I take to be a joke.

8 Tierra Y Hombre Sauvignon Blanc 2018 £7.00

Perennial Casablanca wine has bracing freshness as well as the special warm ripeness of Chilean Sauvignon with asparagus notes and a lemon lift; 12.5% alcohol.

9 Pintao Viognier 2018 £9.00

I'm pleased to see my note on and rating of this new vintage chime entirely with last year's report on the 2017. Plump but fresh and articulate apricot-nectarine fruit in delicious balance with 13.5% alcohol. Dry, distinctive wine to match tricky fish dishes, creamy sauces and salads. New Lower Price of £9 is down rather parsimoniously from £9.50.

WHITE WINES

9 **Val de Loire Sauvignon Blanc 2018** £7.00
Sauvignon from its natural home, the maritime green
landscape of the Loire estuary, is glitteringly fresh, grassy
and crisp with a lush lick of fruit ripeness and just 11.5%
alcohol.

8 **Picpoul de Pinet 2018** £8.00
Newly sourced example of the popular Mediterranean
oyster-matcher has good colour, lemon perfume and a
basket of crunchy white fruit flavours; 13% alcohol.

8 **Bourgogne Chardonnay 2017** £9.00
From the hugely productive Buxy co-op in the Chalonnais
a well-coloured and well-ripened sweet-apple food white
(shellfish to poultry) well balanced between lush and
fresh; 13% alcohol.

9 **Côte de Charme Sauvignon Blanc 2018** £9.00
In the southern reaches of the Loire near La Rochelle the
alluringly named Côte de Charme is new territory to me.
This is a lushly complex and pebbly-bright Sauvignon
somehow comparable to the style of Sancerre, and worth
the acquaintance; 11.5% alcohol.

8 **Alsace Gewürztraminer 2017** £10.00
From the Cave de Beblenheim (winemaker Patrick Le
Bastard) a well-conceived fat rather than sweet Gewürz
with exotic, spicy lychee fruit in nice balance with the
trim citrus acidity; 12.5% alcohol.

WHITE WINES

FRANCE

7   Denbies English White Lily 2018   £10.00

I can see you might buy a bottle from the estate shop on a visit to this splendid Surrey enterprise, but paying a tenner for this at M&S when the same money would obtain some of the brilliant imported wines described here just doesn't make sense. It's a healthy dry country-wine style aperitif with 11.5% alcohol.

10   Réserve du Boulas Côtes du Rhône Villages 2018   £10.00

White Rhône wines are the coming thing, and here's a proper pioneer. It's as rich in orchard and tropical fruit perfumes as it is in gold colour, and lusciously complex (seven different grape varieties in the blend) in its flavours, all trimly defined with citrus acidity; lavish (but no oak contact) and balanced, generous (14% alcohol) but fresh. A discovery.

9   Pouilly Fumé Mathilde de Favray 2018   £17.00

Alluring blossomy bloom on this Loire classic translates into authentic river-fresh Sauvignon flavours of real force; 13.5% alcohol. Top wine at a top price.

GREECE

8   Atlantis Santorini 2017   £12.00

This is the vintage I tasted and liked last year. Is it not selling? It's an exotic dry fresh wine of likeable salinity and 13% alcohol, somehow redolent of its apocalyptic provenance – vineyards on the caldera of Thera, a vast volcano that blew itself to pieces 3,500 years ago, obliterating civilisations and changing the climate.

WHITE WINES

10 Soave Classico 2018 £7.00

Now this is the real thing (see wine immediately above), with fine green-shot-with-gold colour, floral but tangy aroma and a stimulating hit of green acidity on first sip, turning to grassy lushness of crisp white fruits revealing white-nut richness and lemon zest in tandem; 12.5% alcohol. Fab rendering of a classic Verona style, and all at a New Lower Price.

8 Garganega Pinot Grigio 2018 £7.00

Veneto dry wine has only 15% PG along with the Garganega of Soave renown. It has much of the brassica-citrus-blanched-almond style of the better kind of Soave and I liked it; 12.5% alcohol.

8 Gavi Quadro Sei 2018 £8.00

From Piedmont giant Araldica a fresh, even bracing, variation on the fashionable Gavi theme showing crisp green apple crunchiness with a saucy lick of almondy richness; 12.5% alcohol.

8 Craft 3 Marlborough Sauvignon Blanc 2018 £10.00

Healthy silage smell from this appropriately grassy pure varietal is really quite alluring, and the interest continues through the racy, long fruit flavours; 13% alcohol. At a New Lower Price, fair value.

8 Saint Clair James Sinclair Sauvignon Blanc 2018 £15.00

A treat to taste this grand wine from a famous Marlborough winery; it's very fully flavoured (gooseberry, grassy-nettly) and long with glitter and balance in the best Kiwi style. Special occasion aperitif with 13% alcohol, apparently at a New Lower Price.

ITALY

NEW ZEALAND

WHITE WINES

PORTUGAL

8 **Tapada de Villar Vinho Verde 2018** £7.00
The 'green wine' of Portugal's Minho Valley is still the nation's best-known white, but far from its most inspiring. This one's OK, not too oversweetened (the real thing is eyewateringly tart) with a little trace of spritz and lemon lift; 10.5% alcohol.

8 **Journey's End Honeycomb**
Chardonnay 2018 £8.00
Honey is elusive in the panoply of fresh flavours that make up this generous Stellenbosch varietal. Crisp brassica and ripe apple to the fore; 13.5% alcohol and a New Lower Price.

SOUTH AFRICA

8 **Craft 3 Chenin Blanc 2018** £10.00
Stellenbosch wine is almost austere by usual Chenin Blanc standards, but the freshness is very attractive and there's a leesy quality to the stone-fruit heft; a fine balancing act and 13.5% alcohol. Good aperitif and a nice match for shellfish.

WHITE WINES

9 **Candelilla Albariño 2018** £9.00

Spiky green flavours in this terrific new M&S wine by Rias Baixas co-op Martin Codax evoke the seagrass I imagine sprouting from the windswept dunes along the nearby Atlantic shore. It's a big style, but well-lit by citrus acidity, and a major treat matched to fishy dishes of every kind; 13% alcohol.

8 **Jordi Miró White Grenache 2018** £9.00

Pear-blossom perfume and a bright, peach-pear fruit of pleasing weight mark out this intriguing dry wine from Terra Alta, the emerging DO next door to mysterious Priorat in the lost Catalan hinterland; 13.5% alcohol.

FORTIFIED WINES

8 **Late Bottled Vintage Port** £13.00

Grippingly delicious 2012 wine made for M&S by esteemed Taylor's is darkly sweet and spicy with rich black fruit and long, ardent flavours; 20% alcohol.

8 **Manzanilla Sherry** £7.00

Quite a full style to this tangy-briny refresher from fabled seaside sherry town Sanlucar de Barrameda by bodega Williams & Humbert. Crisp and very pale, serve cold; 15% alcohol. New Lower Price.

SPARKLING WINES

8 La Dame en Rose Sparkling 2018 £9.00
Several new sparklers at M&S include this delicately pale
shell-pink rosé from the Languedoc; sweet red-summer-
fruit perfume, soft but persistent sparkle and cleanly crisp
from Carignan grapes in the 'brut' style; 12% alcohol.

8 Champagne Delacourt Brut £30.00
The new house champagne is pleasingly mellow with a
crisp red-apple fruit and lasting flavours; 12.5% alcohol.
The standard price is clearly high compared to the best
supermarket own-brands, but I have noted occasional
discounts up of to a third on this and the companion
vintage and 'medium dry' Delacourts.

7 Prosecco £10.00
House prosecco is safe enough, if not cheap, with plenty
of fizz in the white peary fruit and in the dry style; 11%
alcohol.

9 M&S Cava Brut £7.00
Upfront lemon twang on nose and fruit of this nuanced
Catalan wine; it's fully sparkling and fully fruity too with
orchardy crispness and sunny ripeness; 11.5% alcohol.
So much more fun and better value than prosecco – and
not just M&S prosecco.

Morrisons

Morrisons has style. Among its Big Four rivals it might lack Tesco's leviathan might, Sainsbury's rakish flair or Asda's radical chic. But it produces more of its own goods than any of the others. The stores are smart but somehow down-to-earth, and I believe have the most cheerful and helpful staff. Morrisons has been popularly voted the best chain and in 2019 a new megastore in Cambridgeshire was named the best in the world.

Or something like that. Morrisons' likeability is evident, and real. And this goes absolutely for the wines. The Morrisons wine team are knowledgeable, enthusiastic and good-humoured, and their wines follow suit.

Italian wines are inspired, with a new vintage of Morrisons' own Toscana 'supertuscan' Chianti-style red scoring top marks this year and likewise a mature Barbera d'Asti at only £6.50 which lives entirely up to its own-brand designation 'The Best'.

It's a great year for Rioja in several of the supermarkets but Morrisons pips all the competition with its lavish oxidative white 'The Best Rioja Blanca Reserva 2015' at a cool £13.00. I've been waiting years for a revival of this once rightly popular classic wine style, and this one is a peach. 'The Best Rioja Reserva 2012', incidentally, is also a top scorer among the red wines.

France, Italy and Spain contribute the most to Morrisons' genuinely outstanding wine range, but there are some pleasant surprises among the South African and Argentinian sections. Take time to ponder them in a comforting store near you.

RED WINES

ARGENTINA

8 **Morrisons Malbec 2018** £4.50

Friendly densely flavoured party wine has a trace of Malbec muscularity to give it a pleasing fruit-acidity balance; 13% alcohol.

9 **The Best Gran Montaña Malbec 2017** £7.98

Expansive velvety Mendoza wine by top producer Catena has hallmark Malbec sinew and spice nicely in the background to the abounding ripe blackberry fruit; 13% alcohol.

9 **Viñalba Patagonia Malbec 2017** £10.00

Remarkable seared-fruit winter wine has Malbec darkness and a spicy-sleek lift that might derive from the portion of Syrah in the mix; luxury cushiony oak is evident but not dominant; 14.5% alcohol.

AUSTRALIA

8 **Workshop Bench Blend Merlot 2013** £6.75

Unexpected sweetly ripe and still vivid bitter-cherry fruit in this positively ancient oak-fermented wine is likeable and interesting; 14.5% alcohol. Drink now. Not for keeping.

8 **The Best Margaret River Shiraz 2017** £7.00

Couldn't help liking the toffee richness in this long-flavoured varietal, fermented in oak but lively and juicy in its fruit; 14% alcohol.

8 **Botham All-rounder Cabernet Sauvignon 2017** £7.75

Beefy's very own new Cabernet is wholesome and rounded with good fruit clarity, all at a believable price; 13% alcohol.

RED WINES

9 Morrisons Merlot 2018   £4.50
I think this is an object lesson in making affordable
'entry-level' wine. Credible flavours of healthy ripeness
and balance, true to Merlot's black-cherry juiciness;
12.5% alcohol.

CHILE

8 The Best Carmenère 2018   £7.75
Distinctive bramble-cassis fruit with creamy vanilla
background has the right carmine colour and reassuring
weight; 13.5% alcohol.

8 Cono Sur Reserva Pinot Noir 2016   £9.50
Handsome garnet colour, emphatic cherry-raspberry fruit,
and minty Chilean warmth are all signature qualities in
this enduring global brand; safe, satisfying and 14%
alcohol, a very adaptable food match.

10 Raoul Clerget Beaujolais 2018   £5.00
Last year I awarded 10 to Morrisons' own-label Beaujolais
at a fiver and this brand at the same price is its equal.
Handsome purple-ruby colour and perky-berry aroma from
the joyously juicy fruit are all in perfect alignment at a ripe
13% alcohol. There's even an appreciable grab of acidity at
the finish, suggesting a wine of serious intent. Top buy.

FRANCE

8 Morrisons Côtes du Rhône 2017   £5.00
Warm spicy savour to this above-average party wine,
with noticeable intensity of fruit and a welcome abrasion
at the finish; 13% alcohol.

8 The Best Red Burgundy 2017   £6.40
Pale but interesting colour and a nose offering lemon
twang as well as Pinot Noir raspberry (there's also one
third Gamay in the mix) this is a crisply fruity generic
wine at a very low price, for burgundy; 12.5% alcohol.

RED WINES

8 **The Best Bordeaux Supérieur 2016** £6.75
Mostly Merlot everyday claret from a good vintage now coming round, this has appreciable heft and density of blackcurrant fruit; 13% alcohol.

10 **The Best Languedoc 2016** £7.75
From the vineyard empire of former French rugby international Gérard Bertrand, this amazing contrivance has dense, mellowing colour, wild garrigue aromas and sleek spiciness with reassuring grip and 13.5% alcohol. It is entirely beguiling, even if I can't quite explain it. Tastes way above price.

8 **Vinus By Paul Mas Malbec 2017** £8.25
A Languedoc riposte to all that Argentine Malbec no doubt, and a powerful one. Deep inky colour, spicy-smoky nose and majorly ripe black fruit with the grape's hallmark charred savour; 13.5% alcohol.

8 **The Best Crozes-Hermitage 2017** £9.00
Blueberry aroma to this sturdy purple northern Rhône Syrah translates into vigorous black-fruit flavours with good intensity and grip; 13.5% alcohol. True to this appellation's distinctive style.

8 **Château Treytins**
Lalande-de-Pomerol 2017 £15.00
From a recondite appellation of Bordeaux's right bank, a precocious single-estate claret with a sweet-chestnut richness to its glossy mainly Merlot fruit, it tastes even more expensive than it is and will develop for years yet; 13% alcohol.

RED WINES

ITALY

9 **Sorso Montepulciano 2017** £6.00
Gleefully bouncy, briary and gripping Abruzzo wine with generous ripeness at a very friendly price; 13% alcohol.

10 **The Best Barbera d'Asti 2016** £6.50
As with most Barbera d'Asti in the supermarkets, it's by Piedmont colossus Araldica, but I loved this vividly sweet-briary and juicy pasta red just the same; it has a good heft, 14.5% alcohol and the benefit of years, and looks cheap at this price.

9 **Morrisons Organic Montepulciano 2018** £6.75
The needlessly folksy brown-paper label on this worthy Abruzzo wine undersells it. Briskly brambly with proper juiciness, it's fresh and endearing and equal in value to the Sorso brand above, 12.5% alcohol.

8 **The Best Primitivo 2018** £7.50
Splendidly dark and dense Puglia wine has a kind of fruits-of-the-forest savour to its resounding ripeness; 13.5% alcohol.

8 **Morrisons Nerello Mascalese 2017** £7.50
The 2016 vintage of this distinctive Sicilian pasta red was sensational. This feels less exciting, but I noticed a great improvement on retasting my near-full bottle (bought for just £6 on promo) the day after, so do give it some air. Juicy blueberry fruits in a middleweight frame; 13% alcohol.

9 **The Best Chianti Classico 2015** £8.25
A classic Chianti indeed, this has the most inviting perfume evoking textbook cherry-plummy-briar fruits and following up with lush flavours made slick and complex by oak ageing; 12.5% alcohol.

RED WINES

ITALY

🍷 **10 The Best Toscana 2017** £8.25

Like the Chianti Classico above, this is made by San Felice, a really rather grand estate near Siena. It's classified a humble IGT, but is a proverbial 'Supertuscan' comprising three parts Sangiovese (Chianti's own grape), three Cabernet Sauvignon, one Merlot and two Pugnitello, a variety lately revived by San Felice. Outcome: a lush, intense, wholly Tuscan de luxe wine of seriousness that brings joy and delight; 12.5% alcohol. A must-try, and a great bargain.

🍷 **8 Fontanafredda Barolo 2014** £22.00

The estate of Fontanafredda was founded in 1878 by one of the countless children of Victor Emmanuel II, first king of Italy. The wines were once dull but are now royally good. This limpid lovely gives off an authentic spirity tar'n'roses perfume and delivers sleek, powerful but courtly Nebbiolo flavours – at an appropriately stately price; 13.5% alcohol. In only 100 stores and a real conversation piece.

PORTUGAL

🍷 **9 The Best Douro Red 2016** £7.50

Bumper table red from the vertiginous valleys of the Douro river, home to Port. You get much of the fiery perfume of the fortified wine in this intense ripe blend from the best Port grapes, and a pleasing plumpness of dark spicy fruit too, made silky with oak contact; 13.5% alcohol.

SOUTH AFRICA

🍷 **8 The Best Fairtrade Cabernet Sauvignon 2017** £7.25

I liked the stalky savour to the oak-smoothed ripeness of this gently peppery and nicely rounded Swartland pure varietal made under the Fairtrade scheme; 14% alcohol.

🍷 **8 Granite Earth Red 2017** £8.50

Substantial smooth-running (but unoaked) spicy blend of Midi varieties from the hard-rock vineyards of Swartland is satisfying, wholesome and balanced; 14% alcohol.

RED WINES

8 Castillo del Sabio Tempranillo 2015   £6.00
Mature but unoaked Rioja-style VdT has sweetly insinuating cassis flavours in respectable balance; 13.5% alcohol. Easy-drinking party red.

9 The Best Priorat 2016   £10.00
The red wines of Priorat are known for a 'minerality' said to be imparted by the slaty soils of the steeply terraced vineyards that characterise this lately rediscovered enclave of Catalonia. The appeal is hard to delineate but undoubtedly real, exemplified in wines like this brooding, slick, plummy-blackberry heavyweight at 14.5% alcohol.

10 The Best Rioja Gran Reserva 2012   £12.00
Easily the best of Morrisons' own Best Riojas, it's by Baron de Ley, a much-esteemed bodega whose wines now figure among the own-labels of several leading supermarkets. On the day, this tasted glorious: seductive cassis-butterscotch aromas, poised and bright juicy blackcurrant fruit delightfully nuanced, taut clean finish; 14% alcohol.

PINK WINES

7 L'Escarpe Coteaux d'Aix en Provence Rosé 2018   £8.75
Restrained shell-pink colour, polite floral-red-fruit nose and delicate dry-finishing flavours crisp at the edge and 12.5% alcohol. Identikit Provence pink at what seems to be an inevitable price point.

8 The Best Côtes de Provence Rosé 2018   £9.25
Pale copper-pink and with aromas I imagine akin to strawberry leaves, it has plenty of summer-soft-fruit ripeness and keen freshness finishing very dry; 13% alcohol.

SPAIN

FRANCE

PINK WINES

FRANCE

🍷 8 **Miraval Provence Rosé 2018**   £17.00
Vanishingly pale but emphatically fresh and pink-tasting
celebrity wine from an estate owned jointly, but, er,
separately, by actors Brad Pitt and Angelina Jolie. Although
outrageously expensive, it's a terrific poised, pink-tasting
and crisply brightening wine and a lot of fun; 13% alcohol.

ITALY

🍷 7 **The Best Pinot Grigio Rosé 2018**   £7.25
I don't incline much to either PG or pink wine, but this
was the best of no fewer than four PG rosés kindly offered
for tasting by Morrisons. From Trentino in Alpine Italy, it
has some salmon colour, a suggestion of smoke and fresh
red fruit; 12% alcohol.

🍷 8 **San Marzano Rosé di Primitivo 2018**   £9.25
Pink Primitivo is a new one to me, and this Puglian
novelty exploits the vigorous plum/prune style of the
characterful red wine to make an onion-skin-coloured,
aromatic and full-flavoured rosé with plenty of poke, but
fresh and balanced too; 12.5% alcohol.

WHITE WINES

ARGENTINA

🍷 9 **The Best Uco Valley Chardonnay 2017**   £8.50
Seductively ripe peach-nectarine pure varietal has
expensive creamy richness from partial oak ageing but
all in orderly balance with the liveliness and lemon lift of
the fruit; 13% alcohol. A try by maker La Agricola at the
white-burgundy style, I'd say, and a good effort.

AUSTRALIA

🍷 8 **Jim Barry Watervale Riesling 2018**   £14.00
Top-drawer Riesling from the grape's natural Aussie habitat,
the Clare Valley, this is big in zingy fruit, limey in tang and
luscious as well as racy; 12% alcohol. A contemplative
luxury aperitif or an assertive match for Asian dishes.

WHITE WINES

AUSTRIA

🍷 9   **The Best Grüner Veltliner 2017**   £8.25
The name means green grape from Veltlin (a village in the Austrian Tyrol) and it is the nation's flagship variety. This lushly refreshing example has typical spiciness and minerality with herbaceous notes, quite dry and 12.5% alcohol. A fine aperitif but forever being recommended as a match for 'Asian' cuisine.

CHILE

🍷 8   **The Best Chilean Chardonnay 2018**   £7.25
Peachy fruit is artfully contrived by Casablanca giant Cono Sur in this unoaked but really quite succulent dry generic wine; 13.5% alcohol.

🍷 8   **The Best Muscadet Sur Lie 2018**   £7.50
Stalwart Loire-estuary bone-dry moules-matcher can be eyewateringly tart but this one's easy to like, green and briny in the proper way but ripe and leesy besides; 12% alcohol.

FRANCE

🍷 8   **The Best Touraine Sauvignon Blanc 2018** £7.75
Straight tangy seagrass Loire Sauvignon has real depth of fruit and stands out from the crowd; 13% alcohol.

🍷 8   **Pomerols Picpoul de Pinet 2018**   £8.00
Popular Mediterranean shellfish wine is crisply fresh with agreeable salinity to the eager orchard white fruit; 13% alcohol.

🍷 8   **The Best Alsace Pinot Gris 2017**   £8.25
Rich colour, spicy-smoky nose and ample peach-pear fruit weighted with autumnal ripeness proceed in stately order to the nifty citrus edges of this epic Alsace wine; 13% alcohol.

WHITE WINES

9 The Best Vouvray 2017 £8.75

Rightly respected classic Loire Chenin Blanc is hardly ubiquitous in the supermarkets, so seek this one out if you enjoy honeyed aromas, luscious sweet-white-fruit flavours and poised balance of twangy citrus zest; 12% alcohol. Fine aperitif and a match too for poultry, lobster, creamy cheese and all sorts.

9 The Best Pouilly-Fumé 2018 £12.00

Lemon entry to the flavour of this lushly grassy Loire Sauvignon (neighbour to Sancerre) strikes a nifty counterpoint to the delectably saline ripeness of the fruit; special wine from the heartland of the Sauvignon phenomenon; 12.5% alcohol.

8 The Best Sancerre 2017 £13.00

Proper pebbly-fresh classic Loire pure Sauvignon has welcome evocations of brassica, redcurrant, nettle and citrus; 12.5% alcohol.

9 The Best Chablis 1er Cru 2015 £15.00

Chablis is mythically renowned for its gold-shot-with-green colour, which certainly applies here – and also to the flinty Chardonnay flavours with their lick of richness from the inclusion of some oak-matured wine in the mix. Grand wine from excellent La Chablisienne co-op; 13% alcohol.

8 Bouchard Père et Fils Puligny Montrachet 2017 £36.00

I don't get to taste wine like this very often. It's a Côte de Beaune Chardonnay from one of Burgundy's great appellations made by the biggest vineyard owner in the region, already evolved, fat and opulent with sweet baked-apple fruit but poised, mineral and fresh; 13.5% alcohol. Very nice wine at a price, sold in just 40 of the biggest stores.

WHITE WINES

Ⓨ 8 **The Best Riesling Trocken 2018**   £8.25
Trocken means dry but this delicate aperitif wine from the
Rheinpfalz has a sweet, floral perfume to its crisp apple
fruit with its citrus tang of acidity; a fine and refreshing
balancing act; 12.5% alcohol.

Ⓨ 8 **Sorso Fiano 2018**   £6.00
The fashion for Fiano, an aromatic grape of ancient
lineage, has faded a bit but here's a happy reminder of its
crisp-apple, honey-hinting charm from the enterprising
Settesoli winery at Menfi, Sicily; 12.5% alcohol.

Ⓨ 8 **The Best Trentino Pinot Grigio 2018**   £6.75
Good idea to make it plain on the label that this PG hails
from the foothills of the Alps, where, in Italy, the grape
seems to prosper best. This has smoky notes in the crisp
orchard fruits and a keen citrus lift; 12.5% alcohol.

Ⓨ 8 **The Best Falanghina 2018**   £7.00
Signature white grape of the Campania, the countryside
of Naples, this is an authentic tangy brisk dry white of
character, featuring citrus and even quince in its flavour
range; 13% alcohol.

Ⓨ 8 **The Best Gavi 2018**   £7.50
Almost austere on first taste, this nevertheless has lots of
brassica-herbaceous interest in the crisp white fruit that is
proving such a pull for this growingly popular Piedmont
dry wine; 12.5% alcohol.

Ⓨ 9 **Minea Greco di Tufo 2017**   £8.75
Nuanced Campania dry white from a grape first planted
in the region by ancient Greek settlers in soil composed
of volcanic waste (tufo) does have a certain, possibly
imaginary, brimstone spiciness; it's also crisp, fresh and
lemony-tangy; 12.5% alcohol. Versatile food matcher.

WHITE WINES

8 **Morrisons Pinot Grigio 2017** £4.25
Northern Italy, supposedly the cradle of Pinot Grigio, hasn't exactly distinguished itself in PG production quality, so don't be afraid to look elsewhere – for example a few hundred miles due east to Moldova, whence cometh this fresh and friendly variation at a sensible price; 12.5% alcohol.

8 **The Best Marlborough Sauvignon Blanc 2018** £8.25
Crunchy green sweet pepper and asparagus emerge from the basket of vegetable flavours encapsulated in the aromas and flavours of this dependable pure varietal by esteemed Yealands Estate; 12.5% alcohol.

10 **Klein Street Grenache Blanc 2018** £6.50
I went hook, line and sinker for this fine fish-partner from the Wellington & Paarl region of the Cape. It has attractive colour, aromas of exotic blooms and herbaceous depths to the sweet apple-pear flavours, crisp but craftily rich – there's a bit of Chenin Blanc in with the Grenache and some oak-matured wine in the mix too; 13%. A fine contrivance at a very good price.

8 **The Best Chenin Blanc 2018** £6.75
Gold-coloured Swartland just-dry wine is delicately poised between honeyed ripeness and tangy citrus lift; 13% alcohol. Elegant aperitif.

WHITE WINES

SOUTH AFRICA

🍷 8 The Best South African Sauvignon Blanc 2018 £6.75

On its day, Cape Sauvignon can be equal to Kiwi for interest and value. This well-priced refresher is particularly zesty and lushly ripe besides; 13% alcohol.

🍷 8 The Best Fairtrade Chardonnay 2018 £7.50

Sweetly ripe apple fruit is lively and crisp in this Swartland dry wine, showing good typicity of Chardonnay; 13% alcohol. Unoaked and a simple pleasure.

SPAIN

🍷 10 The Best Rioja Blanca Reserva 2015 £13.00

At last! An old-fashioned oaked and even oxidative white Rioja. Colour going gold, sweet flowery-vanilla nose, ripe matching fruit, creamy but with enduring freshness; 12.5% alcohol. Made by excellent Baron de Ley and fairly priced, if you're a fan of this sort of thing. Do not confuse with Morrison's The Best Rioja Blanca 2018 at £7.75, a mere modern device.

FORTIFIED WINES

SPAIN

🍷 9 Morrison's Fino Sherry £5.75

Bought this in a rush to cook with (Nigella's chorizo-based Spanish Stew if you need to know) and discovered a gem; vanishingly pale colour, tangy-pungent honk and crisp, bright, uplifting bone-dry fruit; made by eminent bodega Emilio Lustau, it's ludicrously cheap; 15% alcohol. Serve well chilled and finish up in a day or two to get all the freshness.

SPARKLING WINES

ENGLAND

8 **The Best English Sparkling Brut** £20.00

By picturesque producer Rolling Green Hills of Sussex, it's from the Champagne grape mix, mainly Chardonnay, convincingly put together, slightly green, and at a price close to credible; 12% alcohol.

7 **The Best English Sparkling
Vintage 2010 Brut** £25.00

Fascinating to taste this immediately after the non-vintage wine from the same source, as it seemed to me unnoticeably further developed than the younger wine, even after more than seven years in bottle; 12% alcohol.

FRANCE

9 **Adrien Chopin Champagne Brut** £18.00

I liked this last year and like it even better this year. The principal among its attractions is its mellowness, as if it has slumbered long in the bottle. A blanc de noir – no Chardonnay in the mix – it's ripe but bright and fresh; 12% alcohol.

9 **The Best Champagne Brut** £19.00

Inviting bakery aromas from this generous non-vintage wine by Louis Kremer lead into a creamy flow of very fine bubbles lifted by a clear lemony acidity – it's really rather good; 12% alcohol. Terribly dreary label lets it down a bit, I think.

ITALY

8 **The Best Prosecco** £7.50

It's pretty brisk, certainly fizzy, and finishes dry with some detectable pear-fruit interest en route. If you must drink prosecco, it might as well be this one, at this sensible price; 11% alcohol.

Sainsbury's

First things first. I have finally checked with Sainsbury's about wine promotions. You know the kind: 25 per cent off everything if you buy six or more bottles at a time. These throw up some brilliant bargains and even include wines on individual discount, almost halving some prices.

Whenever Sainsbury's puts one of these on, Tesco seems to follow suit. Or it might be the other way round. Is this a reactive process, I asked one of the Sainsbury's wine team at this year's tasting, or is it coincidence? Coincidence, I was firmly told. It takes two months to plan these nationwide in-store events and it is simply not possible to replicate a rival's actions in a matter of days.

So there. My informant did concede that the promotions, which are announced at the time of launch, usually via TV and press advertising, are mostly planned for Easter, Christmas, bank holidays and so on. But Sainsbury's intends in future to do them at other less predictable times as well. Yes, in hope of stealing a march on Tesco, and other rivals. What sort of times? Ah, better not say, my confidential source tells me.

Scottish readers will know that these promotions are banned north of the border. Sorry about that.

And so to the wines. Good as ever this year. The Taste the Difference range continues to lead the way.

The glorious 2018 growing and harvesting conditions have enabled the first TTD English Rosé – fine but very expensive – and perennial favourite TTD Côtes du Rhône Blanc 2018 is a top scorer. From the same year but climatically unrelated TTD South African Pinotage 2018 gets maximum points and is one of several Fairtrade wines to stand out.

Red Rhônes are still mostly from 2016 and 2017 – both great vintages in their own right – but do look out for 2018s as they arrive. My favourite French red comes from the neighbouring appellation of Cahors, now enjoying a revival thanks to the craze for its key grape variety the Malbec: Taste the Difference Château Les Bouysses Cahors 2016 is one of the wines of the year. Price is £13.00 but keep alert for the next promo – it could come at any time.

RED WINES

9 SO Organic Malbec 2018 £7.50

The 'SO' in the name might sound a bit camp, but this inky and juicy Mendoza wine is a perennial favourite, always wholesome and true to the spicy-plummy Malbec style; a small part of the blend is oak-aged and the creaminess is evident; very ripe with 15% alcohol but in balance.

8 Zurriago Malbec 2018 £8.00

Dark, warmly spicy and typical in savour, a particularly friendly Malbec with just enough tannin to hold its shape; 14% alcohol.

10 Taste the Difference Morador Malbec 2018 £8.50

Completing a triumphant trio from Argentina, a nicely contrived Fairtrade wine that could well stand as a benchmark for Andean Malbec. It's dark and toastily oaked, spicy but richly padded in texture and ideally weighted, with 13.5% alcohol. A proper crowd-pleaser at a very fair price.

8 Sullivan's Creek Merlot 2018 £5.25

Sullivan is presumably the bloke on the label puffing on a pipe, but this political incorrectness is the least of this very decent party black-fruit red's merits – it's sweetly ripe but healthily balanced; 13% alcohol.

9 Taste the Difference Langhorne Creek Cabernet Sauvignon 2017 £7.50

Deep ruby colour to this pleasingly plump Cabernet is echoed in profound classic cassis flavours arranged in convincing balance of fruit and acidity; modern Aussie wine perfectly expressing what the Cabernet can do Down Under in the right hands, all at a very friendly price; 14% alcohol.

ARGENTINA

AUSTRALIA

RED WINES

8 **Josef Chromy Roaring Beach**
Pinot Noir 2018 £14.50

Handsome limpid ruby colour is untypical of Pinot Noir, but this is Tasmanian Pinot Noir, cherry-raspberry-bright but quite hefty with sunny ripeness, earthy, savoury and long, with a reported precise 13.8% alcohol.

9 **Penfolds Max Cabernet Sauvignon 2016** £19.75

Near-black opaque colour, roasty-toasty ripeness (but not overripeness) and sumptuous cassis fruit kept elegantly poised as much in the (modern) Bordeaux manner as in the traditions of Australia, a senior wine from a great producer at what seems a modest enough price; 14.5% alcohol. Special occasion wine stocked in no fewer than 350 Sainsbury's stores.

8 **Taste the Difference Zweigelt 2017** £9.00

You might never have heard of it, but the Zweigelt is Austria's most-widely planted black grape variety. In this wine it gives dramatically dark intense colour, a sun-baked brambly pong and crunchily perky matching fruit, bright, pure and very dry; 13% alcohol. Nice match for rich foods.

8 **Laughing Llama Merlot 2018** £5.00

Not sure about the branding, but this is pretty good for the money – rounded black cherry fruit kept healthily tight by retained tannin; 13.5% alcohol.

8 **Taste the Difference Maipo Cabernet**
Sauvignon 2017 £9.00

Ignore the odd, fussy label style and relish the cool blackcurrant sleekness of this cushiony but keenly defined natural-tasting pure varietal; 14% alcohol.

RED WINES

9 Taste the Difference Languedoc
Red 2018   £8.00
Convincing maroon colour, similarly winning briar-spice darkly ripe aromas and grippy hedgerow black fruits; consistently interesting and satisfying Mediterranean food red from ubiquitous Jean-Claude Mas; 13.5% alcohol.

8 Taste the Difference Côtes du Rhône
Villages 2017   £8.25
Dependable solid spicy part-oaked 50/50 Grenache/Syrah blend is satisfying in weight and savour; 13.5% alcohol.

8 Taste the Difference Saint
Chinian 2016   £9.00
The same vintage I tasted and described in last year's edition. Is it not selling? It's certainly not mellowing with time, seeming quite tough in its dark, toasty spiciness; 14% alcohol.

8 Taste the Difference Côtes du
Ventoux 2017   £10.00
From the pleasingly alliterative volcanic vineyards of Mont Ventoux in the Vaucluse (actually the conic hill just looks volcanic, it's no such thing) this has a distinct flame-grilled char to the intense spicy briary fruit and unsurprisingly 15% alcohol. Brace yourself.

8 Taste the Difference Pic St Loup 2017   £11.00
The price has moved up from the £9.00 of the magnificent 2016 for this first vintage under the new Pic St Loup AP. This was spicily dark and briary, maybe a bit sinewy, distinctively relishable but in need of time, I'd guess; 13.5% alcohol.

FRANCE

RED WINES

FRANCE

10 Taste the Difference Château Les Bouysses Cahors 2016 £13.00

Last year I gave 9 points to the 2015 vintage at £10.75. The price has risen alarmingly for the 2016 but I'm top-scoring it anyway because this just has to be tried (wait for a 25% promo if necessary). The colour, very deep crimson, could almost be imagined black as in the old and largely imaginary tradition of 'black' Cahors wine. The scent is gorgeous blackberry concentrate, creamy with vanilla oak contact, and the fruit plush, pruny-plummy-cassis-peppery, the lot, all in miraculous harmony in its hefty un-eco posh bottle; 13.5% alcohol. It says here there's 10% Merlot in the mix. Maybe that's the secret.

ITALY

9 Taste the Difference Primitivo 2018 £7.00

Perpetually pleasing Salento IGT wine feels better than ever in this new vintage: dark savour of smooth and fleetingly sweet but grippy plummy-cherry fruit with bright juiciness and a proper cut of acidity; truly wholesome and satisfying pasta-pizza red; 13.5% alcohol. It's often on promo at £6 so my bottle from a 25% off for any six deal cost just £4.50.

8 Taste the Difference Barbera d'Asti 2017 £8.50

Best vintage of this hardy perennial I've tasted in a long time; it has a convincing dark violet colour, sweet cherry-redcurrant nose and tingly red-berry start to the flavour, turning juicily plump in the mouth and closing with a gently gripping firmness; 14% alcohol.

RED WINES

ITALY

Ⴑ 8 **Taste the Difference Marzemino 2018** £8.50
Bottle featuring nostalgic railway-poster-style landscape
scenery suspiciously resembles Asda's Wine Atlas own-
label series (in anticipation of now-doomed union with
Sainsbury's?) but it's a very likeable juicy red-berry
middleweight with brisk acidity and a fine match for
pasta and risotto; 12.5% alcohol.

Ⴑ 9 **Taste the Difference Valpolicella**
Ripasso 2016 £11.00
Darkly rich but not-overblown Verona specialty wine
made with the addition of concentrated grape must is
perfectly judged and fairly priced. Black-cherry fruit
in abundance with notes of coffee, caramel and prune;
13.5% alcohol.

Ⴑ 9 **Ricossa Barolo 2014** £18.00
Don't be deterred by the dull presentation of this special
wine – it's a treat. Limpid colour is going appealingly
tawny, the rose-petal perfume is strong and alluring
and the fruit dances with red-berry savours cloaked in
a lushly oaked richness; there's a retained grip of tannin
and perfect clean finish; 13.5% alcohol.

NEW ZEALAND

Ⴑ 8 **Ara Select Blocks Pinot Noir 2018** £14.00
Pale cherry colour belies abundant ripeness of this
crunchy but silky classic Kiwi Pinot creamily matured
in oak casks; very nicely contrived and fair value; 13%
alcohol.

RED WINES

PORTUGAL

 **9 Taste the Difference Portuguese
Lisboa Red 2017** £7.00

Thoroughly Portuguese in style with hallmark minty-clovey savour to the sleek black fruit, this is from grapes more usual in Douro wines, grown in Atlantic-facing vineyards near Lisbon; it's a winning formula: creamy but gripping cassis-blackberry ripeness, tight clean finish; 13.5% alcohol.

 **8 Feuerheerd's Red Reserva Port
Finish 2015** £11.00

The bottle comes in a brown paper wrapper (handy gimmick for the gift market – Father's Day comes to mind) and the wine, a proper DOC Douro, looks and smells very like Port, as it would, having been matured for a year in old Port pipes (big casks); it's respectable table wine, minty, acceptably raisiny and not oversweet; 13.5% alcohol and innocent fun.

SOUTH AFRICA

 **10 Taste the Difference South African
Pinotage 2018** £7.50

My first top score to a Pinotage, and it's a Fairtrade wine into the bargain. While this grape can make some dull and rubbery wines, this time the typical roasty dark savours are integrated, wholesome and spicily stimulating, enriched by artful oak ageing and finely balanced for acidity; 14% alcohol.

**8 Beefsteak Club Braai Edition
Malbec 2018** £7.50

Presumably a tilt at Argentine dominance in the bovine Malbec market, this is a very decent attempt at the roasty and well, meaty, delights of the celebrated grape; it's darkly, spicily black-fruity and I will forgive the back-label claim of its 'biltong savoury finish'; 13.5% alcohol.

RED WINES

8 Taste the Difference Viñedos
Barrihuelo Rioja Crianza 2016 £7.75
Endearing sweet-vanilla nose invites you into this nicely maturing ripely blackcurrant middleweight wine with all the right Rioja hallmarks by giant bodega Muriel; 13.5% alcohol. Also sold in dinky 187ml bottles (quarters) at £2.50.

9 Condado de Haza Crianza 2015 £15.00
Splendidly opaque blood-red Ribera de Duero pure Tempranillo from the makers of the region's legendary Tinto Pesquera is intense in its creamy cassis fruit, silky, minty-spicy and opulently weighted; 14% alcohol. Delicious now it will probably develop for years. Regularly on individual discount but fairly priced as it is.

PINK WINES

7 Taste the Difference English Rosé 2018 £11.00
Shell pink dry wine from Denbies in Surrey (great visitor experience) it's light in weight and discreet in its pinkly fruity flavours; 11% alcohol. Objectively, it looks madly overpriced.

8 Taste the Difference Fronton
Negrette Rosé 2018 £7.00
Plenty of sweet strawberry scent, and a trace of corresponding flavour, in this coral-coloured dry wine from Negrette grapes grown on home ground at Fronton north of Toulouse; 12.5% alcohol.

PINK WINES

🍷 8 **Taste the Difference Touraine Rosé 2018**   £7.00
Bracingly dry salmon-coloured Loire wine is made
from a mix of Gamay (the Beaujolais grape) and Loire-
red-stalwart Cabernet Franc; upshot is a distinctive
bouncingly bright refresher; 12.5% alcohol.

🍷 8 **Taste the Difference Côtes de
Provence Rosé 2018**   £9.75
Attractive pale copper-pink colour and floral scent lead
on to healthy summer-soft-red-fruit flushes of flavour in a
dry, fresh medium; 12.5% alcohol. Safe bet.

🍷 8 **Taste the Difference Barrihuelo
Rioja Rosado 2018**   £7.50
Strong pink colour and clear cassis aromas and fruit from
Tempranillo grapes make this a recognisably Rioja-style
rosé – and there's no harm in that; 13% alcohol.

WHITE WINES

🍷 8 **Taste the Difference Grüner
Veltliner 2018**   £8.25
Broad exotic flavours build as you savour this intriguing
dry, gently spicy variation on the theme of Austria's rising
star; versatile food matcher and a fine aperitif; 12%
alcohol.

🍷 8 **Taste the Difference Austrian
Riesling 2018**   £8.75
Lemon gold in colour and bright with citrus aroma, it's a
different animal from the delicate Rieslings of Germany,
more like the weightier style of Alsace, but mineral,
natural-tasting and distinctively dry; well worth getting
acquainted with; 12.5% alcohol.

WHITE WINES

CHILE

8 Veleros Leyda Sauvignon Blanc 2018   £10.00
Keenly citrussy and perhaps untypical Chilean variation
has expansive asparagus and seagrass flavours that make
a big impression; 12.5% alcohol.

**9 Taste the Difference Bordeaux
Sauvignon Blanc 2018**   £7.00
The dry Sauvignons of Bordeaux were once identified
simply as Bordeaux Blanc – no mention of the grape. But
now amid the Sauvignon vogue, the variety is writ large.
This one's sea-fresh, grassy and crisp, full of refreshment
and interest – a fine 'expression' of the grape; 12.5%
alcohol.

**9 Taste the Difference Languedoc
Blanc 2018**   £7.50
Another fresh fruit-salad vintage of this hardy annual,
consistently nuanced orchard-to-tropical fruit flavours
with sunny ripeness and rewardingly refreshing at a
doggedly maintained good-value price; flagship wine;
13% alcohol.

FRANCE

**10 Taste the Difference Côtes du
Rhône Blanc 2018**   £8.00
The Viognier and Roussanne that make up half of this
blend (the rest is Grenache Blanc) are aged awhile in oak
casks. I'm telling you this because it might help explain
why this is such a beguiling construct: floral honeyed
aromas, nectarine balance of ripeness (13% alcohol) and
acidity, complex, artfully fresh, dry and vivid.

WHITE WINES

9 Taste the Difference Muscadet de
Sèvre at Maine 2018   £8.00
Textbook Muscadet *sur lie* has the right intensity of sea-fresh green-fruit tang without too much tart acidity (it was a very sunny ripening season in the Loire estuary in 2018) so this one stands out from the crowd; very dry but not fierce and a fine shellfish match; 12% alcohol.

8 Taste the Difference Alsace
Gewürztraminer 2017   £8.99
Big yellow lychee, pineapple 'n' spice aperitif wine is plump and exotic but stays clear of cloying sweetness, finishing brisk; good intro to a classic style; 13.5% alcohol. Good overnight keeper.

8 Taste the Difference Jurançon Sec 2018   £9.00
Jurançon is not yet a household name, but this Pyrenean enclave makes fascinating white wines from local varieties Gros and Petit Manseng (sound like a Gallic comedy duo?) such as this tropically lush yet brisk and edgy dry blend to match big-flavoured fish dishes, salads and all kinds of sunny-day picnic items; 13% alcohol.

9 Taste the Difference Vouvray 2018   £9.50
I suppose I'd have to position this at the sweeter end of the Loire Chenin Blanc scale but its honeyed ambrosial richness is so beautifully balanced by citrus vivacity that the word sweet seems vulgar and redundant; if you like this style you'll love it; 12.5% alcohol.

WHITE WINES

9 **Taste the Difference Petit Chablis 2018** £10.50
The humblest of the four appellations of Chablis reportedly faces extinction but there are still plenty of good wines being made thus classified. This has true gunflint savour to the mineral Chardonnay fruit and long, slaking flavours; a grand treat at a reasonable price for Chablis of any description; 12% alcohol.

8 **Collection Terroirs Riesling 2018** £11.00
From ubiquitous Alsace co-op Cave de Türckheim an untypical rendering of the customary sebaceous Rieslings of the region; from terroirs including 'granite soils, sand, pebbles and limestone' it has an almost green raciness with plenty of citrus zing and long, long flavours; 12.5% alcohol.

8 **Taste the Difference Côtes de Jura**
Chardonnay 2016 £11.00
You can't help admiring Sainsbury's for including a curiosity like this in their flagship range. From the Jura in France's far east, it's a skier's wine, Chardonnay with an extra boot of spice and intensity from grapes grown in the mountainous region's splendid limestone terroir around Arbois; distinctive and likeable wine; 12% alcohol.

9 **Taste the Difference Pouilly Fumé 2018** £13.00
Clearly carefully made new vintage of a consistent Sainsbury's marvel, this is excitingly ripe and expressive of lush pebble-fresh Sauvignon fruit very much in the best traditions of the appellation; 13% alcohol.

WHITE WINES

FRANCE

🍷 8 **Taste the Difference Pouilly-Fuissé 2017** £18.50
High-fallutin' Mâconnais easily confused with Pouilly-Fumé
(see immediately preceding wine) but of course a southern
Burgundy Chardonnay rather than a Loire Sauvignon.
This has fine colour, succulent peachy fruit and hallmark
minerality with a crisp apple-citrus acidity; 13% alcohol.

🍷 8 **Taste the Difference Pinot Grigio
Trentino 2018**   £7.00
Trentino is a sub-Alpine region of Italy and makes livelier
PG than its principal production zones further south. This
one has a fun sweet-cabbage aroma and comes through
fresh, fleetingly smoky and with a lick of white-nut
creaminess; really not bad; 12.5% alcohol. Maybe the
15% Chardonnay in the mix has something to do with it.

🍷 8 **Taste the Difference Vernaccia di San
Gimignano 2018**   £8.00
The famed Tuscan hilltown should be as famous for its
hanging gardens as it is for those soaring towers, and
here's an indigenous wine that pays appropriate homage:
florally perfumed with lush herbaceous notes to the ripe
white fruits, mineral, fresh and uplifting; 12.5% alcohol.

ITALY

🍷 10 **Taste the Difference Greco di Tufo 2017** £10.00
Campania wine labelled with a beautiful illustration
of a Greek amphora in tribute to the ancient origins of
the Greco grape has a fine gold colour, spicy and herbal
scents and flavours echoing apricots and apples, melon
and peach, all rooted in the tufo, the volcanic soil of the
region's sun-baked landscape. An exotic and enticing
dry wine with freshness and zest as well as fascination
and versatility as a food matcher – creamy pastas, fish,
poultry, strong cheeses; 12.5% alcohol.

WHITE WINES

NEW ZEALAND

8 Taste the Difference Coolwater Bay
Sauvignon Blanc 2018 £8.00
Peapod Marlborough wine is brimming with ripeness and
grassy-nettly savour; not subtle and none the worse for
it – loud and clear; 12.7% alcohol.

8 Ara Select Organic Sauvignon
Blanc 2018 £12.00
Part of this blend from Marlborough's Wairau Valley is
'fermented wild to promote more of a textual style' and
another part is 'fermented in barrel to promote oak driven
aromatics'. Contemplate these measures as you savour
the plump grassy lushness of this ripe (13.5% alcohol) de
luxe Kiwi wine.

PORTUGAL

8 Taste the Difference Portuguese
Alvarinho 2018 £7.50
Alvarinho is the same grape as the Albariño, now a buzz
variety in Spain's Rias Baixas region, just north from
where this wine is made in Portugal. It's less hefty and
saline than its Spanish counterpart but lively, lemony and
crisp; 12.5% alcohol.

SPAIN

8 Taste the Difference Barrihuelo
Rioja Blanco 2018 £8.00
Little bit of sweet mintiness gives interest to this modern-
style fresh and dry-finishing white Rioja entirely vinified
in stainless steel tanks, with no ageing in oak; 13%
alcohol.

Sainsbury's

WHITE WINES

 **8 Marques de la Concordia Tempranillo
Blanco 2018**   **£12.00**

SPAIN

This is from vineyards in the Rioja Alta, 'high above sea level, where the cooling effects of the Atlantic Ocean result in slow-ripened grapes with a high flavour concentration and an excellent level of acidity' says Sainsbury's. Well, I liked it, in spite of the price, and can see what they're saying. It's not traditional white Rioja, which is made from Viura grapes, but it does have a racy, crisp lemony – even sea-breezy – vivacity all its own; 12.5% alcohol.

**9 Taste the Difference Californian
White 2017**   **£10.00**

USA

Aged in oak barrels, some new, it's half Chardonnay, with the rest made up of the sort of grape varieties that go into dry white Rhône wines. The effect is a beguiling balance of peachiness, tropical and orchard fruits and artful minerality with 13.5% alcohol. Who would guess it came from California? Really fun and an adaptable food matcher.

SPARKLING WINES

8 Taste the Difference Crémant de Loire   **£11.50**

Made largely with the Chenin Blanc grape, it has a friendly trace of honey amid the brisk, brut fruit style; fine alternative to prosecco if not champagne; 12.5% alcohol.

FRANCE

**10 Sainsbury's Blanc de Noirs
Champagne Brut**   **£19.00**

I can't fault this. It is consistently mellow in colour, bready aromas and lasting fruit flavours; I am even warming to the arty new label, which seems deliberately to camouflage the Sainsbury name, as if this were more than a mere supermarket fizz, which is fair enough; 12% alcohol. Also in magnum at £38.00 and in halves at £12.50.

Tesco

 There's a lot of good wine at Tesco. The range has been steadily cut back over recent years and I still mourn the closure of the dedicated online wine service, but the offering on shelf is rational, diverse and well-priced. Promotions continue frequently.

More than ever, the 'Finest' wines set the pace. Global brands like Barefoot, Hardy and Yellow Tail still persist, but the quality, interest and value are almost entirely owned by Tesco's consistently excellent own-label range. Nine out of ten of the wines I've picked out this year are Tesco's own.

Among the bargains is Tesco Beaujolais 2018 at £5.00, a fine harbinger of what has been a fortuitous vintage not just in Beaujolais and the rest of France, but pretty well Continent-wide. There is even a decent Finest English White 2018, but at £12.00 it is hardly on a par for value with equivalent dry whites from France, Italy and Spain at prices starting from just above £4.00.

Top reds include an early arrival from 2018, Max Chapoutier's thrilling Côtes du Rhône Villages at £9.00 and a positively precocious 2018 Rioja under Tesco's dependable Viña del Cura name at the mad price of £5.00.

There have been very few new wines this year but one I liked is Finest Aromático 2018 from Chile at £8.00; it's a blend of Chardonnay with a mix of

Gewürztraminer, Sauvignon and Viognier, and works surprisingly well.

New World wines figure more widely. I think the Finest Yarra Valley Chardonnay 2018 at £11.00 is delicious evidence that Australia still has mastery of this fine, if diminishingly fashionable, grape variety. Finest San Antonio Pinot Noir 2017 at £9.00 is similarly a reminder that Chile can make world-class Pinot at prices that seem on another planet from those of Burgundy.

RED WINES

ARGENTINA

♟ 8 **Tesco Argentinian Malbec 2018** £5.00
Easy-going Mendoza wine has a bite of dark ripeness
amid the yielding juicy fruit; adaptable party red at a keen
price; 13% alcohol.

♟ 9 **Finest Trilogy Malbec 2016** £12.00
Dense inky beetroot colour, briary smoky aromas and a
big, friendly attack of darkly savoury fruit in this long and
gripping Mendoza wine by local legend Catena; 13.5%
alcohol. Unusually, you are notified on the back label of
this handsome-looking package that you can keep it for
up to three years. Good advice.

♟ 8 **Finest Angelica Sur Malbec 2016** £18.00
For Argentinophiles who like to show off, a lush and
slinky pure varietal with a distinct toasty ripeness from
the cool-climate Uco Valley; 13.5% alcohol. Very nice
turn, at a price.

AUSTRALIA

♟ 8 **Tesco Australian Merlot 2018** £4.25
Modern Merlot for moth-wallets is pale to look at but
healthily plump with dark-cherry fruit in trim balance;
13.5% alcohol.

♟ 8 **Finest GSM 2016** £9.00
It stands for Grenache, Shiraz and Mourvèdre but there's
also a little Cabernet Sauvignon in the mix. It comes out
a bit like Châteauneuf du Pape, only denser and darker,
without being overblown; ripe (14.5% alcohol), spicy
and satisfying it's made by Chester Osborn of d'Arenberg.

RED WINES

CHILE

9 **Finest San Antonio Pinot Noir 2017** £9.00
Made by Cono Sur, a subsidiary of Chilean wine giant
Concha y Toro, it's a big, earthy wine plump with New
World ripeness but made very much in the Burgundian
tradition, complete with a year's ageing in French oak casks;
14% alcohol and a fine match with poultry and game birds.

8 **Finest Peumo Carmenère 2017** £9.00
The carmine colour that names the grape is just about
identifiable (crimson, really) and it has a distinct black-cherry
and blackberry savour, smoothed by oak contact, of its own.
Made by Chile's giant Concha y Toro, but a substantial and
balanced varietal of character; 13.5% alcohol.

FRANCE

9 **Tesco Beaujolais 2018** £5.00
I miss the cheery floral labels of old, but this juicy, jiggly
purple glugger from yet another triumphant Beaujolais
vintage is as much a joy as ever, and a gift at this price;
12.5% alcohol. Did you know sales of Beaujolais in the
UK were up 35% between 2018 and 2019? Wines like
this one are, I'm sure, responsible.

9 **Tesco Comté Tolosan Malbec 2018** £5.00
Terrific bargain from a relatively obscure regional IGP of
the deep southwest, this has a jolly inky mauve colour,
wild blackberry nose and the dark 'leathery' savour
of ripe Malbec; an honest unoaked varietal for meaty
occasions at a gift of a price; 12.5% alcohol.

9 **Tesco Beaujolais-Villages 2018** £7.00
A meaningful step up from the £5 basic Beaujolais (see
above), it has plenty of juicy bounce but with a palpable
and delicious fruit intensity as well, finishing with a nice
grip of tannin; 13% alcohol. Makes a nifty match for
summery meals.

RED WINES

8 Finest Malbec Cahors 2016   £7.50

It seems light at first look and taste but there's a resolute spicy black-fruit savour here that draws you in to the melange of hedgerow and plum flavours; 13% alcohol.

**8 Palais St Vigni Côtes du Rhône
Villages 2017**   £8.00

Rugged Mediterranean cassoulet red in a natty Empire-style package (though with a screwcap) has decent intensity and spice; 13.5% alcohol. Look out for it on promo – I paid £6.00. Not an overnight keeper.

10 Finest Minervois La Livinière 2016   £9.00

Lavish blackhearted Syrah-led Mediterranean monster (14.5% alcohol) comes in a hefty deluxe bottle complete with deep punt and delivers a lot of muscular but silky black-cherry aroma and fruit. It has what might be called a New World kind of cushiony upholstery but the trim is definitely French. Made (some of the blend by carbonic maceration, the Beaujolais method, for juicy bounce) by giant producer Les Grands Chais, but a wine of genuine regional character.

**10 M Chapoutier Côtes du Rhône
Villages 2018**   £9.00

Thrilling heavyweight by famed biodynamic grower est 1808 from a hugely ripe vintage already relishably succulent; deepest maroon, dense cushiony but gently grippy black fruits and a very satisying heft; 14.5% alcohol. Price looks a giveaway.

RED WINES

FRANCE

9 **Finest Lussac Saint-Emilion 2017** £9.00

My pick of Tesco's really good current collection of clarets is dark, slinky and lush with spiced cassis fruit already smoothly developed and satisfying; 12.5% alcohol. Affordable Bordeaux in the modern manner by impressive producer Yvon Mau.

8 **Corbières Castelmaure 2016** £9.00

Generic Languedoc wine looks a dated package but is artfully made with a blend of maceration carbonique (Beaujolais method) Carignan with Grenache and Syrah to make a lively but intense compote of black-fruit flavours with a plush creamy richness; 13% alcohol.

8 **Finest Faugères 2018** £9.00

From the wild far southwest, a darkly spicy garrigue winter red vigorous but not callow in its blackberry fruitiness; 13.5% alcohol. Drink now for bright juiciness or keep for mellow developments.

8 **Finest Médoc 2016** £9.00

Even match of Cabernet and Merlot in this yeoman claret by enterprising Yvon Mau delivers much of the generous ripeness and elegant balance you should expect from the great Bordeaux vintage of 2016; 14% alcohol. Needs a couple more years in bottle, though.

8 **Finest Gigondas 2016** £14.00

You do pay a premium for anything labelled Gigondas, the first among the southern Rhône's little claque of individual village appellations. This one's worth it, brimming with bumper hedgerow-fruit flavours, warmly spicy, and very trim at the finish; 14% alcohol. Good with starchy-meaty combos such as cassoulet.

RED WINES

FRANCE

🍷 8 **Château des Fougères Clos Montesquieu La Raison Graves 2009** £15.00

In supermarkets you don't see many wines from the Graves district south of Bordeaux, and few if any from a fine old vintage such as 2009. This handsome-looking package is in its lusciously gamey maturity and really quite good value; 14% alcohol.

🍷 8 **Finest Margaux 2015** £21.00

New source for this flagship Finest is Château Cazauviel, a less-vaunted estate than former fountainhead, classed-growth Boyd-Cantenac. But it's nevertheless a lovely dense claret with trademark Margaux perfume – cassis, violets, liquorice, vanilla and so on – in fine balance; 12.5% alcohol. Already 'approachable' but years will elevate it higher, I reckon.

ITALY

🍷 9 **Tesco Montepulciano d'Abruzzo 2017** £4.75

Hardy perennial is agreeably plump and briary in this vintage but still with the trademark juicy bounce that gives it a rare refreshment value and happy partner for pizza and pasta; 12.5% alcohol. The price seems gratuitously low for this sort of quality.

🍷 8 **Finest Lambrusco Reggiano Amabile** £7.00

If you haven't yet discovered the mildly fizzy delights of the Emilia-Romagna's Lambrusco here's a friendly introduction: sweetish but cherry-bright and stimulating. For old hands, an authentic wine in the amabile style at 8% alcohol. Serve very cold.

RED WINES

8 **Casa Roscoli Nero d'Avola Sicilia 2017**   £8.00
Regularly discounted to £6, this eye-catching organic
varietal (vegan even) in terracotta-coloured livery has a
good pruny grip to the baked-ripe black fruit and plenty of
woof (13.5% alcohol). Better value at £6 than £8 and not
an overnight keeper.

8 **Finest Chianti Classico Riserva 2010**   £8.00
Nicely presented mature wine by heavyweight Melini
winery is surprisingly lively for its age, less nuanced than the
excellent 2009 it succeeds, but still generous with trademark
Chianti sour-cherry tang along with rounded richness;
13.5% alcohol. I picked one up for £6 on promo.

9 **Sette Muri Brindisi Riserva 2015**   £10.00
Silky and balanced heel-of-Italy Negroamaro in a fancy
bottle has warmly peppery topnotes to the plushly oaked
blackberry/plummy fruit and tidy clean finish; the *sette
muri* are seven of the walls that traditionally flank the
tracks through the Brindisi province's vineyards; 13.5%
alcohol. Good value, especially at the £7.50 I paid on
promo, and a good overnight keeper too.

9 **Finest Valpolicella Ripasso 2017**   £11.00
It can be hard to relate this quaint Veronese wine to the
pale, cherry-bright style of its begetter, Valpolicella. But in
a good one like this, by the esteemed Cantina Valpantena,
you get both the eager charm of the base wine and the
dark velour imparted by contact with grape skins from
the Recioto process. It's wildly and uniquely delicious;
13.5% alcohol.

RED WINES

ITALY

🍷 **8** **Finest Barolo 2014** £16.00

It's from regional giant producer Fratelli Martini, but this is more than mere generic supermarket Barolo. It's pale ruby in the expected way, scented with sweet cherry and rose petal but with a lurking spiritousness that suggests the sinew and grip in the fruit. Yes, it does sound fanciful, but I do fancy this wine – and will do so even more in a year or two after it has come round a bit (as Barolos quite often do); 13.5% alcohol.

🍷 **9** **Finest Amarone della Valpolicella 2016** £18.00

It's coffee pungent and dark-chocolate sweet all at the same time, with a stout-like bitterness amid fruits evoking mulberry, bramble, maybe even sloe. Hard to deconstruct, definitely, but this brooding monster (15.5% alcohol) made from dehydrated Valpolicella grapes by Cantina Valpantena is a huge treat. Big match for red meats and strong cheeses.

NEW ZEALAND

🍷 **8** **Finest Marlborough Pinot Noir 2018** £9.00

Pale garnet colour, cherry-raspberry nose, and bee-sting bright shock of red fruit; very much a Kiwi Pinot, nothing like burgundy, harmless fun; 13% alcohol.

🍷 **9** **Finest Central Otago Pinot Noir 2017** £13.00

Dense colour (for Pinot) and a gripping, near-sinewy and burgundy-like fruit in this satsifyingly serious oak-matured wine with hallmark Kiwi sleekness; 13.5% alcohol. Definitely a wine of character to enjoy with a roast bird; made by formidable Villa Maria.

RED WINES

10 Tesco Douro 2017 £5.75

This delightfully poised table wine from the Port vineyards has the dark, beetrooty look of the famous fortified concoction and even quite a bit of the same spikily savoury aroma. The juicy, minty black fruit has an easy heft (13.5% alcohol) and a friendly grip of warmly spicy tannin. Outstanding at this price.

9 Tesco Viña del Cura Rioja 2018 £5.00

Youthful plump juicy unoaked Rioja is genre-specific and convincingly delicious – a brilliant all-round party wine; 13% alcohol.

9 Tesco Viña del Cura Rioja Crianza 2016 £6.75

Obvious but relishable vanilla lick to this wine by Bodegas Muriel flatters the sweet, eager blackcurrant fruit in a nicely gripping texture; 13.5% alcohol. Very impressive at this price.

8 Finest Viña del Cura Rioja Reserva 2014 £8.50

Perennial favourite by dependable bodega Baron de Ley has a sweet vanilla richness to the keen gently spicy blackcurranty fruit; 13.5% alcohol. Nifty buy, particularly at the oft-discounted price of £6.99. Good overnight keeper. New this year are 50cl bottles of this, at £6.00.

8 Pulpito Toro 2017 £11.00

Pleasingly abrasive and ripe Tempranillo from Toro has the region's hallmark black-pepper savours and substance; ideal match for assertive menus; 13.5% alcohol. In Spain a *pulpito* is a baby octopus, as depicted in the label illustration. Toro is a high-altitude wine zone east of Zamora, very far from the sea, but where famed local dishes include *pulpa a la sanabresa*.

RED WINES

SPAIN

🍷 9 **Finest Viña del Cura Rioja Gran Reserva 2012** £11.00
Lush violet-cream-cassis nose and dark velvet fruit to this still-evolving new vintage (the 2011 scored 10 last year) from Baron de Ley; 13.5% alcohol. I paid £8.80 on promo, which is a giveaway. Good overnight keeper.

PINK WINES

ARGENTINA

🍷 8 **Finest Malbec Rosé 2018** £7.50
Pale and interesting Andes wine is quite dry and fresh with flavours suggesting pomegranate, even apricot – intriguing and likeable; 13% alcohol.

FRANCE

🍷 8 **Tesco Coteaux d'Aix-en-Provence Rosé 2018** £7.00
Shell pink dry aperitif wine has delicate strawberry trace en route to a gently citrus edge; 12.5% alcohol.

SPAIN

🍷 8 **Tesco Tempranillo Garnacha Rosé 2018** £4.50
Magenta colour reveals the bold intent of this heartily fruity strawberry confection from the great wine lake of La Mancha. It's quite dry, but with a lot of ripe fruitiness and 11% alcohol.

WHITE WINES

8 **Tesco Australian Chardonnay 2018** £4.25
Made by renowned Andrew Peace, a ripe and artfully oaky chardy nothing short of fair dinkum, and at a rare bargain price; 12.5% alcohol.

8 **Finest Dessert Semillon 2015** £6.00
Burnt gold colour and honeyed botrytis aromas and flavours to match in this artful contrivance from the Riverina vineyards of De Bortoli. Ingenious balance, 10% alcohol (there's a lot of retained sugar) and very good value. A fine sweet aperitif.

8 **Finest Tingleup Riesling 2018** £9.00
Hardy (well, Howard Park winery) perennial has crunchy red-apple fruit with a grapefruit and lime twang; 12.5% alcohol.

10 **Finest Yarra Valley Chardonnay 2017** £11.00
Richly coloured and just as opulent in its apple-pie-with-cream aromas, you might expect a stonking Aussie brute, but this wine by genius Steve Webber of De Bortoli owes as much to Chablis as it does to chardy of the old school. Its minerality is in perfect harmony with its lush ripeness; I think it's perfect, and worth it; 12.5% alcohol.

8 **Finest Aromático 2018** £8.00
One of just a handful of new Tesco wines this year, it's a crowd-pleasing blend by Cono Sur of Chardonnay, Sauvignon, Gewürztraminer and Viognier; deserves a mention for its artful balance of vegetal-mineral-citrus savour with freshness and fullness; 12.5% alcohol. Aperitif or a match for everything.

WHITE WINES

ENGLAND

7 **Finest English White 2018** £12.00

The peary-appley aromas of the constituent Pinot Blanc and Chardonnay grapes lend this Kentish blend an Alsace-like disposition, which lifts it somewhere above average for a dry English white; nice melange of white fruits and a citrus twang; 11.5% alcohol. But objectively, the price is bonkers.

FRANCE

9 **Tesco Côtes de Gascogne Blanc 2018** £5.25

Very tangy blend of Colombard and Ugni Blanc – once largely cultivated for the base wines that make Gascony's armagnac brandy – evokes Sauvignon Blanc but has its own distinct lemon meringue pie balance of ripe fruit and twang to produce a terrific fresh dry white at a true bargain price; 11% alcohol.

10 **Finest St Mont 2017** £6.50

Benchmark bargain Pyrenees dry white in yet another shining vintage. Glowing autumn colour, aromas of orchard blossom and meadow herbs and a positive fruit salad of ripe, lush flavours make for a proper wine for all seasons. I am perpetually fascinated by the character and quality of this wine and almost equally in wonder at the paucity of its price; 13.5% alcohol.

8 **Finest Picpoul de Pinet 2018** £7.50

Stands out for the fullness of its crisp white fruits as well as for their eagerness; decent rendering of the persistently popular holiday seafood glugger made near Sète on the Mediterranean coast; 13% alcohol.

WHITE WINES

🍷 8 **Finest Alsace Gewürztraminer 2018** £9.00
Rarely, an own-label Gewürz not made by the ubiquitous Türckheim co-op; plenty of colour and lychee perfume, and generous exotic spicy flavours without excessive sweetness; 14% alcohol. It's made by Arthur Metz, part of giant Grands Chais.

🍷 8 **Finest Chablis 2017** £12.00
Authentic gunflint note to this generic wine suggests it's a good prospect for keeping a year or two; crisp, bright and citrussy now; 12.5% alcohol.

🍷 8 **Finest Sauternes 2015 37.5cl** £12.00
Pure-gold honeyed luscious pud wine from a really rated vintage is creamy and toasty but in ideal balance for acidity and freshness; 13% alcohol. Price for this very grand half is perfectly fair.

🍷 8 **Finest Viré-Clessé 2016** £12.00
Lush pure Chardonnay from a new (well, 1998) but prestigious Mâconnais appellation is creamily oaked, luxuriantly ripe and sinfully delicious; 12.5% alcohol.

🍷 9 **Finest Pouilly Fumé 2018** £13.00
It takes only a little imagination to attribute the crystal purity of this fine Sauvignon to the proximity of the great river upon which the little town of Pouilly-sur-Loire so idyllically stands; pebble-fresh and genuinely nuanced, a complex wine worthy of the name; 12.5% alcohol.

WHITE WINES

FRANCE

🍷 8 **Finest Sancerre 2018** £14.00

The AC of Sancerre, just across the river from Pouilly, outshines its rival for renown but they're neck and neck winewise. This well-coloured Sauvignon is as lush as it is mineral, with classic pebbly-nettly-floral savours; 13% alcohol. For what's it's worth, I liked the Pouilly best.

GERMANY

🍷 8 **Tesco Rheinhessen Riesling 2018** £5.00

Noticeable spritz lends additional zest to this simple aperitif wine; convincingly ripe sweet-apple Riesling fruit lifted by crisp citrus acidity; 11% alcohol. Bit of a bargain at a fiver.

🍷 8 **Finest Mosel Riesling 2018** £8.75

Sweetish but wholesome and racy fermented-out modern Riesling for aperitif drinking; 12% alcohol. Dull label doesn't do it justice.

ITALY

🍷 8 **Tesco Frascati 2018** £4.75

The once-fashionable café wine of Rome is happily embodied in this delicately green and tangy refresher, complete with its suggestion of almondy creaminess; 12.5% alcohol.

🍷 8 **Tesco Finest Pecorino 2018** £7.00

Pecorino, cultivated in the mid-eastern province of Abruzzo, could be the new Pinot Grigio. This one has a lush grassiness of real appeal and tangy citrus lift to the fresh green fruits; 13% alcohol.

WHITE WINES

ITALY

🍷 **9**   **Finest Beneventano Greco 2017**   £9.00
Mellow colour to this brisk Campania wine from exotic Greco grapes leads into correspondingly complex savours of stone fruits and herbaceous perfumes; 13% alcohol. It really grows on you, making a fine aperitif as well as a match for poultry dishes, creamy pasta, even pongy cheeses.

NEW ZEALAND

🍷 **8**   **Finest Barrel Reserve Sauvignon Blanc 2018**   £9.00
If you're mystified by the merits claimed for oaked Sauvignon, try this. You do get the nettly-grassy Kiwi style but there's a tropical-fruit lusciousness here that highlights rather than masks the Sauvignon thrill; 13.5% alcohol.

🍷 **8**   **Finest Gisborne Chardonnay 2017**   £9.00
Distinctive Kiwi Chardonnay, all but swept away in the Sauvignon tide, makes a welcome guest appearance in this rather luscious oaked wine delivering long and satisfying peachy-mango flavours lifted by minty citrus acidity; 13.5% alcohol.

PORTUGAL

🍷 **7**   **Tesco Vinho Verde**   £5.25
Pushed off its summer-plonk pedestal by the likes of Picpoul de Pinet, VV struggles for quality and interest these days. This non-vintage cheapie has a trace of spritz, a shade of 'green' tanginess and isn't as oversweetened by residual sugar as some; 10.5% alcohol.

WHITE WINES

SOUTH AFRICA

🍷 8 **Finest Fairtrade Breede River Sauvignon Blanc 2018** £7.50
Straight zesty gooseberry-grassy style with a lick of sunny ripeness to the lasting flavours; 12.5% alcohol.

🍷 8 **Finest Fairtrade South African Chenin Blanc 2018** £7.50
Nectar-bearing spring-blossom nose leads on to zesty orchard fruit with a clear honey note and a near-tart citrus acidity in a fine balancing act; 12.5% alcohol.

🍷 8 **Tesco Spanish Chardonnay 2018** £4.15
Ripe sweet-apple style is unmistakably Chardonnay, and of thoroughly decent quality, trimmed with a neat citrus acidity; 12% alcohol. Remarkable at this price.

SPAIN

🍷 7 **Tesco Viña del Cura Rioja Blanco 2018** £5.25
If you like the modern tart citrussy style of white Rioja you might like this; 12.5% alcohol.

🍷 8 **Finest Viñas del Rey Albariño 2018** £8.50
Zippy Rias Baixas brims with grassy green fruits with a heft of sunny ripeness and eager tangy acidity; 12.5% alcohol.

FORTIFIED WINES

🍷 **8** **Tesco Special Reserve Port** £8.25
Made by ubiquitous Symingtons, a thoroughly wholesome ruby port with sweet mellow fruit and an agreeable fieriness; 20% alcohol.

🍷 **8** **Tesco Finest LBV Port 2013** £10.50
A clear step-up from the Special Reserve above, it's nicely developed but spicily eager and as deep in rich black fruits as it is in intense maroon colour; 20% alcohol.

🍷 **10** **Finest 10-Year-Old Tawny Port** £12.50
Attractive colour is just turning copper and the fruit is mellowing accordingly, blending into the ardent embrace of the spirit creating a fine melange of figgy-nutty sweetness and gentle fieriness; 20% alcohol. Made by Symingtons, an exceptionally good-value rendering of this very approachable style of wood-aged port. Straight from the fridge, it makes a toothsome aperitif.

🍷 **8** **Finest Fino Sherry 37.5cl** £6.00
At £6 for a half it's the same price as grand brands like Tio Pepe, but this pale, bone-dry, tangy-fresh and crisp fino by Gonzalez Byass (who'd have guessed it – the makers of Tio Pepe) is entirely on a par; 15% alcohol. Drink it very cold and don't keep it more than two days after opening. Shouldn't be a problem.

SPARKLING WINES

ENGLAND

8 Finest English Sparkling   £19.00

From busy Kentish vineyard Hush Heath a remarkable achievement. It's made from the same grapes that go into champagne, Chardonnay and Pinots Meunier and Noir and by the 'champagne method' and it tastes just as you would expect of a champagne at this price. It is, in short, a contender; 11.5% alcohol.

8 Finest Blanquette de Limoux 2016   £9.00

The story goes that the sparkling wine of Limoux in the Pyrenees predates champagne by a century; this one fairly jiggles with crisp orchard fruits in its soft persistent mousse, all in a distinctive style of its own (not champagne-like), fresh and friendly, not too dry; 12.5% alcohol.

FRANCE

8 Finest Crémant de Limoux Rosé 2016   £12.00

Companion pink to the fizz immediately above, it's attractively shell-pink in colour, softly sparkling (*crémant*) and endearingly flush with raspberry-strawberry fruit flavours, dry and crisp; 12.5% alcohol.

8 Champagne Louis Delaunay Brut   £14.00

Cheap but by no means nasty non-vintage brand from the delightfully named Marne village of Dizy is lively with lemon twang as well as yeasty richness; price can vary wildly, down as well as up; 12.5% alcohol.

SPARKLING WINES

10 Finest Premier Cru Champagne Brut £20.00

According to Tesco's blurb the Chardonnay grapes (70%) come only from Premier and Grand Cru vineyards at Avize and the Pinot Noir (30%) from exclusively Grand Cru sites at Bouzy and Ambonnay. The wine is largely or entirely from the (outstanding) 2012 vintage. It is correspondingly brilliant, rich in colour, generous, even creamy in mousse and fruit with a warming bakery backdrop and crisply refreshing acuity; 12.5% alcohol. How do they do it?

8 Finest Premier Cru Champagne
Rosé Brut £23.00

From the same winemaker, Cedric Jacopin, responsible for the two excellent 'white' Finest champagnes, this vividly coloured (smoked salmon, I call it) non-vintage fizz has a discreet strawberry scent, busy creamy mousse and bright fruit; tastes pink and tastes like champagne, too; 12.5% alcohol.

9 Finest Vintage Grand Cru Blanc de
Blancs Champagne Brut 2012 £26.00

Long-flavoured mellowing pure Chardonnay from choice vineyards is for keeping, really, if you can bear to wait; it's already rewardingly good and from a much-vaunted vintage, and by no means overpriced; 12.5% alcohol.

SPARKLING WINES

ITALY

8 **Finest Valdobbiadene Prosecco**
Superiore DOCG Brut £10.00
The DOCG Conegliano-Valdobbiadene in the Veneto's
Cartizze district claims to make the best of all Prosecco.
This smartly presented manifestation is unusual in
incorporating a measure of Chardonnay and Pinot Blanc
wine with principal constituent grape Glera. It's softly
frothing, elderflower-scented and ripe-pear fruity, not
really dry enough to warrant the description 'brut' but
agreeable in its way; 11.5% alcohol.

8 **Finest Franciacorta Extra Brut** £15.00
Pure Chardonnay fully fizzing Lombardy sparkler has
bracing appley fruit and reassuring yeasty mellowness;
very likeable indeed and £15 is a small price to pay for
anything bubbly from Italy that isn't prosecco; 12.5%
alcohol.

SPAIN

9 **Tesco Cava Brut** £6.00
Pushy Catalan sparkler made by the traditional
(champagne) method has vigorous mousse and crisp
orchardy white fruit with a brisk freshness; 11.5%
alcohol. Such a bargain compared to pointless prosecco.

Waitrose

 Waitrose & Partners, as we must now call our grandest grocer, is facing challenging times. Profits announced in 2019 were 45 per cent down on the previous year and the Partners, no doubt gratified at the new inclusiveness of the corporate identity, must have been less delighted with their annual bonus of 3 per cent, the lowest since 1953.

At the awe-inspiring Waitrose press tasting this year, I can't say our hosts, the extensive wine team, were looking in any way downcast. Pierpaolo Petrassi, Master of Wine (the first Italian to gain that distinction) and head of buying, was pleased to announce that among the uncountable wines on show on the day, nearly 90 were entirely new to the Waitrose list.

That's as many new wines as I have knowingly tasted across the whole of the rest of the supermarket sector this year. Waitrose is the only multiple (except maybe Aldi) significantly maintaining the scale and diversity of its wine offering, let alone extending it.

Where to start? Italy's a good place. Presumably thanks at least in part to the influence of Snr Petrassi, the Italian range is extraordinary. I have picked out a dozen reds including an unexpectedly delectable Sangiovese from Emilia-Romagna (otherwise known only for Lambrusco) and two prime Primitivo wines from Puglia, Paolo Leo and Terre de Faiano, the latter irresistibly scoring maximum points. The half-dozen

Italian whites include Waitrose's own Blueprint Soave Classico 2018, one of a good few from this in-house range showing well this year.

Red burgundies figure too. Two of my picks are respectively from Rully and Givry in the Chalonnais, a southern outpost of the region not always given its due. The Rully by esteemed grower/merchant Joseph Drouhin is a star, and the Givry from a 1er cru estate Clos de la Marole, is a revelation.

A word about sherry. Waitrose is making alterations. The splendid Solera Jerezano own-label range that used to include all the styles, including Palo Cortado, has disappeared and the offering is now more fragmented. But there is an unfussy-looking Waitrose Medium Dry Amontillado at £7.29 for a 75cl bottle and it is wondrous. If you care about sherry, try it.

And if you care about wine generally, shop at Waitrose. The range is as good ever. The prices are entirely competitive and there are promotions on scores of different wines, changing monthly, regularly including many of those mentioned here.

If you don't have a store nearby, please note that Waitrose Cellar continues as a dedicated wine online service – really the last by-the-individual-bottle one left. It's impressively efficient, delivering as soon as next day. Charge is £5.95 for the normal service but it's free for orders of £150 upwards.

RED WINES

10 Waitrose Blueprint Mendoza Malbec 2018 £7.99
Best of the Waitrose bluebottles tasted on the day, it's inky maroon, wildly, darkly black-fruit perfumed and brimming with toasty rounded warmly spiced fruits in wholesome balance en route to a textbook taut finish; 13% acidity. Model Malbec at a proper price.

9 Norton Coleccion Malbec Lujan de Cuyo 2018 £10.49
Eco-friendly Mendoza wine has rich blackberry-pie flavours and no sharp edges to the darkly roasty fruit, shamelessly commercial and none the worse for that – especially at occasional promo price of just £6.99; 13.5% alcohol.

8 Tilimuqui Fairtrade Organic Malbec 2018 £11.99
Poised and balanced Famatima Valley wine with good social and viticultural credentials has clear oak character but plenty of lively black fruit; 13% alcohol.

8 Botham The All-rounder Cabernet Sauvignon 2018 £7.99
Wholesome balanced recognisably Cabernet wine blended from several SE Australian sites including Coonawarra; I would not describe it as beefy; 13% alcohol. I've seen it on offer at £5.99.

8 Airs and Graces Malbec 2017 £9.49
Avert your eyes from the grim anthropomorphic label art and relish this craftily weighted spicy pure-fruit Victoria wine for its healthy juiciness and natural charm; 13% alcohol.

ARGENTINA

AUSTRALIA

RED WINES

Waitrose (vertical, left margin)

AUSTRALIA (vertical, left margin)

🍷 8 **Botham 80 Series Cabernet Sauvignon 2016** £10.99

It's obviously well-made and does justice to the good name of oak-matured Coonawarra Cabernet, but for the moment it's a bit tough; 14.5% alcohol. Waitrose's weasel words suggest it's 'drinking very well now' with the wise codicil that 'we suggest cellaring this wine for another five to seven years'. Cricket lovers can invest with confidence, I'd guess.

🍷 8 **Irvine Spring Hill Barossa Valley Merlot 2017** £11.99

It's the blithe weight of it that grabs the attention – something like the heft of a very expensive Pomerol Merlot. I liked the black sweet ripeness (14.4% alcohol) and artful balance. Merlot buffs should try this.

🍷 8 **Jim Barry The Forger Shiraz 2016** £24.99

From a famous name in the Clare Valley an extravagant but perfectly poised ready-to-drink long-oak-aged savoury super-silky Shiraz with more than a hint of northern-Rhône Syrah (same grape as Shiraz, as you know) about it. Gorgeous and satisfying for a special occasion; 14.5% alcohol.

FRANCE (vertical, left margin)

🍷 9 **Cuvée Chasseur 2018** £5.49

Wholly dependable Pays d'Hérault is just brilliant in this new vintage: perky eager brambly but rounded Carignan-Grenache fruit is juicy and lasting and in ideal balance; 12.5% alcohol. Extremely modest price has been maintained from last year's excellent vintage.

🍷 9 **Sous le Soleil du Midi Merlot 2018** £5.99

Hallmark black-cherry fruit in this generic Vin de France has appreciable spice and grip perhaps from its unstated home terroir of St Chinian – impressively intense and satisfying for the money; 13.5% alcohol.

RED WINES

🍷 8 **Cuvée des Vignerons Beaujolais** £7.79
Non-vintage Duboeuf-made ordinary Beaujolais is joyfully juicy and ripe if not quite a bargain at this price (look for it on offer at £6.19 though) and full of interest; 12% alcohol.

🍷 9 **Costières de Nîmes L'Arène des Anges 2018** £7.99
The arène is the astonishing Roman amphitheatre still largely intact in the centre of Nîmes and an attraction rightly equal in renown to the town's famous wines; this is a really good one, bold, briary and spicy with an easy weight and vigorous ripeness (14% alcohol) to the distinctive Rhône-country savour.

🍷 8 **Waitrose Blueprint Côtes du Rhône**
Villages 2017 £7.99
Sweet suggestion of oak ageing on this dark and quite intense gently spicy Grenache-Cinsault gives allure to the nose and savour to the fruit; 13% alcohol.

🍷 8 **Calmel & Joseph Villa Blanche Piquepoul**
Noir 2018 £8.49
Hedgerow-fruit Hérault wine is raisiny ripe but nicely grippy and abrading; good starchy food match; 12.5% alcohol. Piquepoul Noir is rarely identified in wines but is closely related to popular white Picpoul of Provence.

🍷 8 **Mme Parmentier Fitou 2016** £8.49
Nostalgic revival of the original 1980s branded Fitou, the Languedoc appellation that largely launched the region's reputation for quality. This is a decent example of the genre, dark, intense and lipsmacking; stands up very well to reopening; 12.5% alcohol. Bought for £6.29 on promo.

RED WINES

7 Remy Ferbras Ventoux 2017   £8.49

Much less weight and savour in this than in the delightfully dark and spicy 2016. Hold out for the 2018 – reportedly yet another vintage of the century for the Rhône.

8 Malbec de Balthazar Pays d'Oc 2018   £8.69

Perky middleweight summer Malbec/Grenache blend evokes sun-baked blackberry on the nose and delivers a juicy gush of brambly fruit; 12.5% alcohol. The £6.49 I paid on promo is closer to the right price for this.

8 Jean-Luc Baldès Malbec du Clos Cahors 2016   £8.99

Yet another Cahors seeking identity by naming its constituent Malbec grape, it has inky colour and a roasty char to the spicy blackberry fruit; it has heft, balance and distinctive character – Cahors and not just in mere name; 13.5% alcohol.

9 Château Queyret-Pouillac 2015   £10.49

Particularly ripe and obligingly developed Merlot-based Bordeaux Supérieur from the Entre-Deux-Mers has long cassis fruit and a firm clean finish; 13.5% alcohol. Look out for occasional promo at £6.99.

10 Château Tour de Gilet 2016   £10.99

Médoc Bordeaux Supérieur has gleaned plenty of fruit depth (70/30 Merlot/Cab Sauv) from the ideal 2016 vintage in the region; it's positively popping with proper briar-cassis-plum ripeness (14% alcohol) and in perfect balance; textbook 21st-century claret.

8 Col de La Serre St Chinian 2015   £11.49

Gamey ripeness and fruits-of-the-forest savour in this beefy red from the redoubtable Cave de Roquebrun make for a winter warmer of real substance; 13% alcohol.

RED WINES

9 Georges Duboeuf Morgon 2015 £11.79
Among the Beaujolais crus, Morgon is said to be the longest lived. Keep it a while and slinky sinew is added to the juicy bounce of the younger wine. This one illustrates the principle perfectly; 13% alcohol. At this price it won't sell fast, but look out for it on promo – I paid £8.79.

10 Côtes du Rhône Guigal 2015 £11.99
Iconic Syrah-dominated wine is entirely perfect in this wonderfully ripe and developed vintage, intense and dark in colour, silky and spicy and perfectly weighted – an 'everyday' CdR in a class of its own; 13.5% alcohol. It could quite easily be mistaken for a very expensive Chateaneuf du Pape. My bottle, bought for £8.99 on promo and recorked half full was as good as gold 48 hours later. Why can't all wine be like this?

8 Bourgogne Pinot Noir Cave de Lugny 2018 £11.99
Unoaked wine from a seriously good Mâconnais co-op amply illustrates the style of the highly rated Burgundy 2018 harvest: hot and dry at the right times. This is full of ripe savour, with a firm grip of tannin; 13% alcohol. No rush.

8 Château Lagrave St Emilion 2015 £14.99
St Emilion on the right bank of Bordeaux's Dordogne river makes claret of a distinctive early-maturing kind but with depths and darknesses all its own; this one from a fine year is rounded and sleek with liquorice and plum evocations and healthy balance; 13.5% alcohol.

8 Cave de St-Désirat Saint-Joseph 2017 £15.99
Admired Northern Rhône appellation's principal co-operative makes this pure Syrah of deep crimson colour, slick peppery blackberry fruit and long, clinging texture finishing bright; 13.5% alcohol.

RED WINES

8 **Domaine St Amant Beaumes-de-Venise**
Grangeneuve 2015 £15.99
From a village of the Côtes du Rhône known for its sweet
whites this muscular deep-maroon monster of mature
vintage is a revelation: wild black berry fruit with garrigue
minty-spicy core is powerful and toothsome; 14.5% alcohol.

9 **Rully Joseph Drouhin 2015** £16.99
Beguiling sweet English-cherry perfume from this limpidly
ruby-coloured slinky Chalonnais Pinot Noir is entirely
fulfilled by the earthy mellow plumply ripe fruit; 12.5%
alcohol. Rustic burgundy of real character.

9 **Givry 1er Cru Clos de la Marole Domaine**
Deliance 2017 £21.99
Givry in the Chalonnais region of southern Burgundy
shows off its undoubted credentials in this scintillating
Pinot Noir of silkiest raspberry ripeness and mineral-like
purity of fruit; it's creamily oaked in new casks but trim
and crisp in its finish; 13% alcohol.

9 **Aloxe Corton 1er Cru Clos des**
Maréchaudes 2015 £47.50
From Beaune producer Albert Bichot's Domaine de
Pavillon – an estate I have visited and greatly liked – this
is lavish burgundy from a great and maturing vintage at
the going price. Shining silky pure Pinot Noir of sublime
ripeness and balance, earthy but elegant, intense but
dancingly other-worldly; 13.5% alcohol. Safe investment
for a very special occasion.

8 **La Piuma Montepulciano d'Abruzzo 2017** £7.99
Longstanding brand at Waitrose has sweet confected nose
but it turns out an agreeably intense brambly mouthfiller
with juicy healthy ripeness and clean dry finish; 13%
alcohol.

RED WINES

🍷 **8** **Recchia Bardolino Veneto 2018** £7.99

Jewel-like light garnet colour, cherry-blossom nose and bright crunchy fresh cherry flavour finishing very dry and brisk all work in happy harmony to make this Verona favourite a delight to drink chilled on summery occasions; 12.5% alcohol.

🍷 **9** **Borgodei Trulli Salice Salentino 2017** £8.99

I had the word 'earthy' in mind before inspecting the back-label blurb on this truly salubrious Puglian spaghetti partner. 'This lovely red wine displays deep earthy aromas of blackcurrants, vanilla and chocolate' the legend goes. Quite so, a textbook mass-market Negroamaro of great character, picked up on promo for a laughable £6.99; 13% alcohol.

🍷 **9** **Montidori Sangiovese 2017** £8.99

Artful confection from the Emilia-Romagna, a region little known for winemaking, this submits the grape of Tuscany's Chianti to the recioto/ripasso method of the Veneto's Valpolicella to make a darkly dense, plump and satisfying spaghetti red. The distinctive pot-like bottle is presumably intended to compensate for its odd provenance and it's good value, especially at the £6.99 I paid on promo; 13% alcohol.

🍷 **9** **Araldica Barbera d'Asti Superiore 2017** £9.49

Lush successor to the 2015 vintage enthusiastically reviewed here in last year's edition, this juicy number features the hallmark blueberry bite of Piedmont's deliciously distinctive Barbera grape; plenty of heft, 14% alcohol and keenly edged; has been on promo at £7.49.

RED WINES

10 Terre di Faiano Primitivo 2017 £9.99
Soupy but ideally weighted organic monster from Salento (Puglia) comes in a hefty bottle emblazoned in glowing orange livery. Sweetly ripe and plump, it nevertheless has a trim cut of acidity; 14% alcohol. Price is perfectly fair but it has been discounted to as little as £6.66 more than once, which makes it an exceptional bargain.

8 Rapitalà Nero d'Avola 2017 £9.99
Nice heft to this warmly ripe indigenous varietal from hill country (as artily illustrated on the label) just south of Sicily's teeming capital Palermo. Toasty blackberry fruit with friendly-grip tannin in the proper style of the Nero grape, said to originate from the seaside town of Avola 200km away on the island's south-east coast; 13.5% alcohol.

8 Sagrato Chianti Riserva 2015 £10.79
It's not worth £10.79 but the £6.99 I paid on promo turned out a decent investment. It's light for a *riserva* but juicily ripe in the perky Chianti tradition, bright with vivid purply fruits and finishes with a nifty nutskin dryness; 12.5% alcohol. Made by giant Cecchi, a wine to drink now, not to keep.

9 Paolo Leo Primitivo di Manduria 2018 £10.99
Plum, cinnamon and sweet black cherry number among the evocations in this big cushiony Salento wine dense with roasty black fruit; deeply savoury but trim and brisk at the finish, a fine balancing act; 14% alcohol.

RED WINES

 9 **Masi Campofiorin Rosso del
Veronese 2016** £12.99

Iconic is an overused encomium but this one-off from Valpolicella producer Masi does merit the description; cushiony plump and as dark in flavour as in colour it delivers the familiar cherry savour of its region with added notes that might remind you of plum, cinnamon, violets and marzipan. It's recognisable even through variations in vintages and dependably ready to drink; price is fair especially at frequent Waitrose discount down to £9.99; 13% alcohol.

 8 **Waitrose Valpolicella Classico Ripasso
Superiore Fratelli Recchia 2016** £12.99

Easy-to-like example of this popular fruit-boosted style from Verona, it's generously ripe and savoury without the raisiny taint that can spoil some of these wines; 14.5% alcohol. At £9.74 on promo, a nice buy.

 8 **Castello di Bossi Chianti Classico 2015** £19.99

Castello di Bossi is a 9th-century estate and Chianti is a 19th-century contrivance; this conceit from 100% Sangiovese (not the classic Chianti recipe) is fabulously grand and mellow, a treat for show-offs; 14% alcohol.

8 **Terre del Barolo 2015** £19.99

Very approachable elegant wine with smoky floral aroma and sleekly oaked maturing slinky red fruit; 14% alcohol.

 **8** **Mud House Pinot Noir 2018** £10.99

On-trend Central Otago wine lives up to the hype. Very ripe and intense with slinky-minty Kiwi-style fruit and only sweet in the pleasingly lingering aftertaste; artful and beguiling; 13% alcohol.

RED WINES

NEW ZEALAND

8 Saint Clair Gimblett Gravels Syrah 2018   £12.99
To look at it you'd think it's Pinot Noir so pale is the colour – nearer magenta than red – but the fruit has the slink and spice of Syrah with the Kiwi twists of rare ripeness and vividness; really interesting and attractive red wine; 12.5% alcohol.

PORTUGAL

9 Gran Passo Classico Tinto 2016   £7.99
This same vintage featured here at the same price and score last year, now just as inkily dark and delicious in the distinctive minty-clovey Portuguese style with a lick of vanilla richness and 14% alcohol. Why hasn't it sold out? Could be the groovy jazz-age-style labelling and screwtop (on a Portuguese wine!) which utterly obscures its origins and manifest charms. A true bargain, especially at the £6.49 I paid on promo.

**8 Quinta do Carmo Dom Martinho
Tinto Alentejo 2017**   £11.99
Lush minty-clovey unoaked full-of-lively-fruit dark thriller from indigenous Portuguese varieties has classic indigenous charms; very full but with a firm tannin grip; 14.5% alcohol. In only 7 stores but available online.

SPAIN

**9 Waitrose Mellow and Fruity Spanish
Red 2018**   £4.99
Consistent warmly savoury and gently spicy party red from Garnacha grapes grown in Campo de Borja region is wholesome and terrific value; 13.5% alcohol.

RED WINES

SPAIN

🍷 8   **Anda Tempranillo-Syrah 2016**   £7.99
Red wine from Andalucia, the province of sherry, is a
pleasant surprise; it's wholesome with cassis flavours and
earthily ripe, not at all like northern Tempranillo wines
including Rioja but with a charm its own; 14% alcohol.
Don't be put off by the heated-looking arty label.

🍷 8   **Jumilla Viña Elena Organic
        Monastrell/Syrah 2017**   £7.99
Versatile food red thanks to the cheerful abrasion of
its vivid briary and wholesome red fruits, this Murcia
wine stands out for thoroughly Spanish exuberance and
vigour; 14.5% alcohol.

🍷 8   **Castillo de Olite Navarra Tinto 2013**   £9.99
Well-developed earthy-truffly sweet-vanilla Tempranillo-
Garnacha from Rioja's overlooked neighbour has mature
charms all its own – not a Rioja clone; eye-catching
package to enjoy now rather than keeping; 13.5%
alcohol.

🍷 8   **Muga Seleccion Especial Rioja
        Reserva 2014**   £24.99
From among a vast choice of Riojas at Waitrose this
extravagance from ubiquitous Muga is a standout. Very
dark callow-looking colour it is still in the process of
marrying the slinky classic Rioja fruit with the vanilla-
rich elements of oak contact and the wait will be worth
it; 14% alcohol.

RED WINES

USA

8 **Drouhin Dundee Hills Pinot Noir 2015**   £36.49
In effect, burgundy from the Pacific northwest of the US in the state of Oregon, made by Véronique Drouhin, scion of a distinguished family of Beaune winemakers who have had vineyards at Dundee Hills since the 1980s. The wine is silky with cherry-raspberry fruit in the best burgundy tradition and spot on for drinking now; 14% alcohol. Expensive, yes, but not by comparison with current prices for the French model.

PINK WINES

ENGLAND

7 **Simpsons Estate Pinot Noir Rosé 2018**   £13.99
Aah, English rosé. From the North Downs of Kent, a nicely coloured very dry wine with traces of raspberry and strawberry in the delicate flavour, clean, bright and expensive; 12.5% alcohol.

FRANCE

8 **Le Rosé de Balthazar 2018**   £6.99
Delicate pink colour to this Pays d'Oc Syrah/Grenache gives way to pleasing summer soft red fruit flavours of convincing freshness; 12.5% alcohol.

8 **Waitrose Blueprint Côtes de Provence
Rosé 2018**   £9.99
Pale salmon colour but lots of brightly pink-tasting ripe fruit – the strawberry tends to denote Grenache, comprising most of this – finishing dry and clean; 12.5% alcohol.

GERMANY

8 **Johann Wolf Pinot Noir Rosé 2018**   £9.99
Near-spritzy zinginess lends life to this salmon-coloured, strawberry-scented dry wine from the Rheinpfalz; 11.5% alcohol. Good Pinot character to the fresh fruit.

PINK WINES

SPAIN

🍷 9 **Marquesa de la Cruz Garnacha Rosé 2018** £7.99
Smoked-salmon colour, clear strawberry brightness in
the fresh, zesty fruit and a determinedly pink character
all round. A generous friendly dry wine from the rarely
mentioned Campo de Borja region; 13.5% alcohol. This
is my idea of rosé, and at the right sort of price (and
sometimes £5.99 on promo).

WHITE WINES

AUSTRIA

🍷 9 **Waitrose Blueprint Grüner Veltliner 2018** £7.99
Sweet blossom perfume is paradoxically partnered
by particularly perky, pungent fruit, finishing dry and
refreshing; 12% alcohol. Standout example of this
surprisingly popular oddity, and at a good price.

ENGLAND

🍷 8 **Waitrose Blueprint English Dry White 2018** £9.49
Made by Surrey outfit Denbies in England's Vintage
of the Century, it is indeed dry but aromatic, too, with
elderflower lending a country note and white-fruit
crispness from the happily retro grape blend of Bacchus,
Ortega et al; 12% alcohol. It's charming and for once
priced below a tenner – which is surely where the future
of English still wine must lie.

🍷 8 **Simpsons Estate Chardonnay 2018** £13.99
From Kent and presumably owing much to the miraculously
warm and sunny conditions of the 2018 growing and
harvest seasons, a proper apple-peach and mineral crisp
Chardonnay comparable with the Mâconnais style; 12.5%
alcohol. Not cheap of course, but maybe a harbinger.

WHITE WINES

9 Cuvée Pêcheur 2018 £5.49
It has green and crunchy orchard-fruit flavours bolstered by sunny ripeness and eased with crafty residual sugar – artfully made Gascon wine at a true bargain price; 11.5% alcohol.

8 Sous le Soleil du Midi Chardonnay 2018 £5.99
Mediterranean dry wine shows clear red-apple Chardonnay fruit substantiated by some oak contact as well as ripeness from what must have been a harvest very much under the sun in 2018; fresh as well as full and 13.5% alcohol.

8 Muscadet La Marinière 2018 £6.49
Brisk and briny lemon-edged Loire bone-dry wine is safely short of tart in its acidity and a nifty match for moules – as indicated in the name; 11.5% alcohol.

8 Waitrose Blueprint Touraine Sauvignon Blanc 2018 £7.99
Cautious Loire wine has likeable Sauvignon grassy tang and appreciable green fruit without any tartness; an artful contrivance to please the many – and why not; 12.5% alcohol.

8 Le Grand Ballon Sauvignon Blanc 2018 £8.99
Generic Loire wine is impressively ripe and leesy, big with grassy-nettly fruit and very clipped at the finish; 12% alcohol.

8 Bourgogne Chardonnay 2018 £9.99
I'm always on the lookout for authentic white burgundy at less than the price of, say, a free-range oven-ready chicken. This new Mâconnais (my guess) wine from the sunniest of vintages will do: pure mineral apple-crisp with stone-fruit ripeness at heart and citrus cut; 13% alcohol. Good with roast chicken!

WHITE WINES

8 Côtes du Rhône Blanc Gabriel Meffre 2018 £9.99
There seems a sudden rush of white CdR – *tant mieux*!
This is a dry one with a basket of fruit flavours taking
in apple, pineapple, mango and grapefruit among others;
teeteringly balanced by a limey acidity; 13% alcohol.

**8 Château Rampeau
Sauvignon/Semillon 2018 £10.49**
Traditional Bordeaux Blanc blend is floral, delicate
and very dry but with a crafty lushness from Semillon's
tropicality and some oak contact with a balancing twang
of citrus; 12% alcohol.

10 Château de Montfort Vouvray 2017 £11.99
Sublime Loire Chenin Blanc labelled 'demi-sec' is as
fresh as it is honeyed, as bright as it is rich, and a hugely
versatile food wine as well as an elegant aperitif. Will
suit chicken dishes, shellfish or salty almonds with equal
aplomb. Seductive floral perfume, meadow-lush and
thrillingly balanced; 12% alcohol. I paid £9.49 on promo
but it's a bargain even at shelf price.

8 Despagne Biface Blanc 2017 £13.49
From the Entre Deux Mers of Bordeaux a 50/50 Sauvignon-
Semillon blend in a grand heavy bottle with other old-
fashioned virtues besides: well-coloured with plump fruit-
salad savours amid the racy and tangy grassiness, but
elegant and delicate all along the way; 12% alcohol.

9 Alsace Gewürztraminer Paul Blanck 2017 £14.99
Fully spicy well coloured lychee scented wine is better
defined than your average supermarket Alsace Gewürz
and in fine balance; it is grapy rather than sweet and has
a natural exotic savour; 13.5% alcohol.

WHITE WINES

FRANCE

8 Domaine Maison Blondelet
Pouilly-Fumé 2018 £15.99
Fine pebbly-fresh Sauvignon from a great Loire appellation
has a seductive floral note in the nettly aromas and fruit;
13.5% alcohol.

9 Pouilly-Fuissé Marc Dudet 2017 £17.99
Pure deliciousness, I've written in my rambling note
on this arrestingly good Chardonnay from a top AC of
Burgundy's southern outpost the Mâconnais. It has the
region's mintily sweet apple-crisp style to a T and offers
lushness and minerality in equal prolixity; 13% alcohol.
See what I mean about rambling?

8 Chablis Domaine Louis Moreau 2018 £17.99
Chablis is getting expensive. This bog-standard AC wine
at a 1er Cru price is a case in point, but it's jolly good:
masses of green-gold colour, archetypical gunflint and
crisp-fruit aroma, long classic Chardonnay fruit (no oak)
flavours with tangy acidity; 12.5% alcohol.

9 Saint-Aubin Premier Cru Domaine
Gérard Thomas 2016 £25.99
To my dismay the only Côte d'Or (heartland, mainstream)
white burgundy I got to taste on the day, but a lovely
one from the Côte de Beaune just the same. Brilliant
lemon-gold colour, floral fleetingly nectareous oaked
Chardonnay aromas, leesy lush fruit of peachy ripeness
and slinky luxury, clipped by lemon lift; 13% alcohol.

GERMANY

8 Waitrose Blueprint Dry German
Riesling 2017 £7.99
Plenty of colour, apple-blossom perfume and matching
crisp fruit in this fresh dry mosel in the modern fermented-
out manner; 12% alcohol.

WHITE WINES

**9 Goldschild Urziger Würzgarten Riesling
  Spätlese 2015**   **£9.49**
Only sold via Waitrose Cellar, this marvellous mosel is
honeyed but scintillating and mineral in its fleetingly
petrolly classic crisp-apple Riesling fruit; 8% alcohol. If
you like real German wine, get online, schnell.

8 Grey Slate Riesling Private Reserve 2017   **£9.99**
From the estimable Ernst of Dr Loosen renown, this is
a fine mineral mosel wine with a peachy ripeness to the
classic Riesling zest; 10.5% alcohol.

**8 Georg Mosbacher Deidesheimer Herrgottsacker
  Riesling Trocken Erste Lage 2017**   **£14.99**
Well-coloured Rheinpfalz wine in the Trocken (dry) style
has generous ripe sweet-apple fruit and emphatic citrus
twang to balance; 12.5% alcohol.

**10 Willi Haag Brauneberger Juffer Sonnenuhr
  Riesling Auslese 2016**   **£19.99**
Among an admirable German flush at Waitrose this
classic mosel is the one I was most hoping for. It didn't
disappoint. The colour is rich gold, the perfume honeyed
but edgy with citrus, the fruit gloriously autumnal with
suggestions of botrytis but racy, lemon-limey-fresh and
defined; 7.5% alcohol. It's rare to find a world-class wine
like this in a supermarket and only six Waitrose branches
stock it but you can buy it online at Waitrose Cellar. Price
is entirely warranted.

8 Soave Cantina di Soave 2018   **£5.69**
Attractive dry lemony typical Veronese stalwart with
freshness and a trace of nutty sweetness; 11.5% alcohol.
Alluring price too.

WHITE WINES

8 Waitrose Blueprint Soave Classico 2018   £6.99
Fuller style, though also authentic, than the bargain Soave above, and more complex in its fruit and brassica message; 12.5% alcohol.

8 Le Stelle Vermentino Sardinia 2018   £8.79
Peachy-tangy dry white from charismatic grape variety Vermentino cultivated on Sardinia's impossibly picturesque sea-facing Antichi Poderi Jerzu vineyard; 13.5% alcohol. Try the wine, visit Sardinia.

8 Marée d'Ione Organic Fiano 218   £8.79
Fiano seems to have fallen from favour of late but here's a welcome reminder, from Puglia, of its elusive charms. Orchard-fruit fresh and crisp with a ghost of honeysuckle in the aromas and a lick of blanched almond in the mouthfeel; 13% alcohol. Is Marée d'Ione the organic winemaker? No. She is the Ionian Sea, which laps the Puglian shore.

8 Fenaroli Pecorino Superiore 2017   £9.99
Unassuming package (no graphics of comical sheep on the label) this is a fine mineral-herbaceous brisk dry Abruzzo wine comfortable with strong cheese or creamy pasta; 13% alcohol. Nice buy on promo at £7.49.

8 Zenato Villa Flora Lugana 2018   £11.99
Reassuring to see this enduring brand from Lake Garda on such good form. Nice floral bloom, expressive ripeness of white and stone fruits in a fine harmony with the lifting citrus acidity; 13% alcohol. Has been on promo at £9.49.

8 La Monetta Gavi del Comune di Gavi 2018 £12.79
Premium wine from a chi-chi Piedmont DOCG is fulsomely ripe with crisp herbaceous white fruits discreetly plumped with blanched-almond creaminess and finishing very dry with a clear citrus edge; 12.5% alcohol.

WHITE WINES

8 **Waitrose Blueprint Marlborough**
Sauvignon Blanc 2018 £7.99
As in Europe, but of course in the opposing half of the
year, there was an especially hot growing season in 2018
in New Zealand. This house wine shows off the ripeness
in its expansive gooseberry aroma, full tangy-nettly fruit
and well-managed lemony edge; 12.5% alcohol.

8 **Crux Sauvignon Blanc 2018** £10.49
Distinct grapefruit note upfront on this untypical
Marlborough wine does set it apart, and leads into really
quite weighty tropical-citrus flavours that linger long on
the palate; 12.5% alcohol.

8 **The Ned Sauvignon Blanc 2018** £10.99
Well-named wine (The Ned is a 909-metre mountain peak
of Marlborough's Waihopai valley) by star winemaker
Brent Maris has quietly become a benchmark Kiwi
Sauvignon, now ubiquitous and frequently on offer; I
paid £7.99 for this one. Really quite lush these days but
still gamely pungent with keen grassy tang; 13% alcohol.

9 **Kaapzicht Kliprug Bush Vine Chenin**
Blanc 2018 £13.99
Rich colour and guava-honeydew aromas lure you quickly
past the bizarre Afrikaaner name of this Stellenbosch
phenomenon into the ambrosial flavours cast by the
magic of the Chenin Blanc grape. Opulent in its white-
fruit glory but also crisply bright and tangy fresh in its
perfect balance; 13% alcohol.

8 **Terra Sagrada Organic White 2018** £6.99
I was really taken with this generic (from the great plain
of La Mancha) dry white from 80/20 Verdejo/Sauvignon
Blanc. Tangy nectarine nose, eager grassy-aromatic fruits,
full of natural (organic?) freshness; 11.5% alcohol.

NEW ZEALAND

SOUTH AFRICA

SPAIN

WHITE WINES

8 **Cune Rioja Blanco 2017** £10.99

Revival of the largely extinct oaked white Rioja style is moderately successful. Labelled as barrel-fermented, it has a good bit of yellow colour and a shade of the oxidative bakiness of the old days, but the main thing is the tropical-fruit richness en route to the artful grapefruity twang; 13% alcohol. Forever on promo typically at £8.79, which is good value.

9 **Palacio de Fefiñanes Albariño Rias Baixas 2018** £15.99

Grandly labelled in the heraldic style, this is a de luxe spin on Galicia's coolest white: bold extracted white-fruit seagrassy flavours lifted by vivid lemon-lime acidity all in a most zesty and sharpeningly refreshing medium; 13.5% alcohol. Aspiring wine from a rightly-admired tradition.

FORTIFIED

9 **JM Fonseca Alambre Moscatel Setubal 2012** £7.99

Gorgeous aperitif wine made by halting the fermentation of super-ripe Moscatel grapes with a shot of spirit has honeyed richness teamed with keen zest in perfect balance; 17% alcohol. Absolute bargain.

7 **Waitrose Reserve Tawny Port** £13.99

This is strictly an aperitif tawny. Keep it in the fridge as the Portuguese do. It is light, though not without full-on sweet fruity charm (made by Symingtons and claimed to be a blend of wines aged seven years in oak) and expensive (mine cost about a tenner on promo); 20% alcohol.

FORTIFIED

🍷 10 Sandeman 20-Year-Old Tawny Port   £39.99
Surely the loveliest port of its kind, the Sandeman is beautifully coloured bronze-copper (and, well, tawny I suppose) and lets you know it by coming most unusually in a clear-glass bottle of the shape that commemorates the shipper's founding in 1790, with a glass stopper. The wine is pure silk, rich and balanced, an object lesson; 20% alcohol. It's expensive but seems perpetually to be on offer in Waitrose at the usefully reduced price of £31.99.

🍷 10 Waitrose Amontillado Medium Dry Sherry £7.29
Newish addition to the much-shaken-up Waitrose own-label sherry range has lovely mahogany colour, defined pungent sweet nut and dried fruit aromas and crisply bright toasty-smoky corresponding flavours; inspired balance of richness and freshness; 18.5% alcohol. The price for this masterpiece of blending is a sure clue to the astonishing undervaluing of sherry.

🍷 9 Waitrose Blueprint Manzanilla Sherry   £7.69
Wild seaside-fresh pong from this delectably pungent and zesty bone-dry sherry; 15% alcohol. Serve ice-cold in decent-sized glasses. Very keen price.

SPARKLING WINES

🍷 8 Bird in Hand Sparkling Pinot Noir   £15.99
Smart package from the Adelaide Hills is just slightly pink, barely rosé in colour, but outgoing in its strawberry-fool Pinot flavours; 12.5% alcohol, refreshing and likeable.

SPARKLING WINES

8 **Prince Alexandre Crémant de Loire Brut** £12.99
Very full apple-crisp leesy fizz does have a proper 'creaming' mousse and delivers a lot of lush fruit flavours, finishing perfectly dry and bright; 13% alcohol.

9 **Cave de Lugny Sparkling Burgundy Blanc de Blancs** £13.99
Crémant de Bourgogne, which this is in all but name – Sparkling Burgundy seems a lot less lyrical – is mostly produced by what used to be called the champagne method in the Mâconnais, where the Cave de Lugny is a major co-operative. This pure Chardonnay is mellow and crisp all at once, not like champagne, but delightfully uplifting, especially at the regular promo price of £10.49; 12% alcohol.

9 **Waitrose Blanc de Noirs Champagne Brut** £22.99
Based on the 2015 vintage but including reserve wines going much farther back this pure Pinot Noir is movingly mellow and calming as well as lively and stimulating; 12% alcohol. Regularly on promo at 20% off.

8 **Waitrose Blanc de Blancs Champagne Brut** £23.99
I cannot fathom why it's always a quid more than the Blanc de Noirs (above) and I still don't like the chilly-looking new blue label, but it's a jolly nice bready pure Chardonnay, mature-tasting and rewarding; 12.5% alcohol.

9 **Waitrose Cava Brut** £9.99
Yeasty and mellow as if bottle-aged a while this non-vintage lively sparkler by Castello Perelada (14th-century estate favoured by Spain's royal family and Salvador Dali too) is full of satisfying flavours, interest and fun; 11.5% alcohol.

Enjoying it

Drink or keep?

Wines from supermarkets should be ready to drink as soon as you get them home. Expensive reds of recent vintage, for example from Bordeaux or the Rhône, sold as seasonal specials, might benefit from a few years' 'cellaring'. If in doubt, look up your purchase on a web vintage chart to check.

Some wines certainly need drinking sooner than others. Dry whites and rosés won't improve with time. Good-quality red wines will happily endure, even improve, for years if they're kept at a constant moderate temperature, preferably away from bright light, and on their sides so corks don't dry out. Supermarkets like to advise us on back labels of red wines to consume the product within a year or two. Pay no attention.

Champagne, including supermarket own-label brands, almost invariably improves with keeping. Evolving at rest is what champagne is all about. Continue the process at home. I like to wait for price promotions, buy in bulk and hoard the booty in smug certainty of a bargain that's also an improving asset. None of this applies to any other kind of sparkling wine – especially prosecco.

Of more immediate urgency is the matter of keeping wine in good condition once you've opened it. Recorked leftovers should last a day, but after that the wine will oxidise, turning stale and sour. There is a variety of wine-saving stopper devices, but I have yet to find one that works. My preferred method is to decant leftovers into a smaller bottle with a pull-cork or screwcap. Top it right up.

Early opening

Is there any point in uncorking a wine in advance to allow it to 'breathe'? Absolutely none. The stale air trapped between the top of the wine and the bottom of the cork (or screwcap) disperses at once and the 1cm circle of liquid exposed will have a negligible response to the atmosphere. Decanting the wine will certainly make a difference, but whether it's a beneficial difference is a matter for conjecture – unless you're decanting to get the wine off its lees or sediment.

Beware trying to warm up an icy bottle of red. If you put it close to a heat source, take the cork out first. As the wine warms, even mildly, it gives off gas that will spoil the flavour if it cannot escape.

Chill factor

White wine, rosé and sparkling wines all need to be cold. It's the law. The degree of chill is a personal choice but icy temperatures can mask the flavours of good wines. Bad wines, on the other hand, might benefit from overchilling. The anaesthetic effect removes the sense of taste.

Red wines can respond well to mild chilling. Beaujolais and stalky reds of the Loire such as Chinon and Saumur are brighter when cool, as is Bardolino from Verona and lighter Pinot Noir from everywhere.

Is it off?

Once there was a plague of 'corked' wine. It's over. Wine bottlers have eliminated most of the causes. Principal among them was TCA or trichloroanisole 123, an infection of the raw material from which corks are made, namely the bark of cork oak trees. New technology developed by firms such as Portuguese cork giant Amorim has finally made all cork taint-free.

TCA spawned an alternative-closure industry that has prospered mightily through the supply of polymer stoppers and screwcaps. The polymer products, although unnecessary now that corks are so reliable, persist. They're pointless: awkward to extract and to reinsert, and allegedly less environmentally friendly than natural corks.

Screwcaps persist too, but they have their merits. They obviate the corkscrew and can be replaced on the bottle. They are recyclable. Keep them on the bottles you take to the bottle bank.

Some closures will, of course, occasionally fail due to material faults or malfunctions in bottling that allow air into the bottle. The dull, sour effects on wine of oxidation are obvious, and you should return any offending bottle to the supplier for a replacement or refund. Supermarkets in my experience are pretty good about this.

Wines that are bad because they are poorly made are a bit more complicated. You might just hate it because it's not to your taste – too sweet or too dry, too dense or too light – in which case, bad luck. But if it has classic (though now rare) faults such as mustiness, a vinegar taint (volatile acidity or acetate), cloudiness or a suspension of particles, don't drink it. Recork it and take it back to the supplier.

Glass action

There is something like a consensus in the wine world about the right kind of drinking glass. It should consist of a clear, tulip-shaped bowl on a comfortably long stem. You hold the glass by the stem so you can admire the colour of the wine and keep the bowl free of fingermarks. The bowl is big enough to hold a sensible quantity of wine at about half full. Good wine glasses have a fine bevelled surface at the rim of the bowl. Cheap glasses have a rolled rim that catches your lip and, I believe, materially diminishes the enjoyment of the wine.

Good wine glasses deserve care. Don't put them in the dishwasher. Over time, they'll craze. To maintain the crystal clarity of glasses wash them in hot soapy water, rinse clean with hot water and dry immediately with a glass cloth kept exclusively for this purpose. Sounds a bit nerdy maybe, but it can make all the difference.

What to eat with it?

When tasting a hundred or more wines one after the other and trying to make lucid notes on each of them, the mind can crave diversion. Besides describing the appearance, aroma and taste, as I'm supposed to do, I often muse on what sort of food the wine might suit.

Some of these whimsical observations make it into the finished reports for this book. Like all the rest of it, they are my own subjective opinion, but maybe they help set the wines in some sort of context.

Conventions such as white wine with fish and red with meat might be antiquated, but they can still inhibit choice. If you only like white wine must you abstain on carnivorous occasions – or go veggie? Obviously not. Much better to give detailed thought to the possibilities, and go in for plenty of experimentation.

Ripe whites from grapes such as Chardonnay can match all white meats, cured meats and barbecued meats, and most saucy meat dishes too. With bloody chunks of red meat, exotic whites from the Rhône Valley or Alsace or oaky Rioja Blanco all come immediately to mind.

As for those who prefer red wine at all times, there are few fish dishes that spurn everything red. Maybe a crab salad or a grilled Dover sole. But as soon as you add sauce, red's back on the menu. Again, the answer is to experiment.

Some foods do present particular difficulties. Nibbles such as salty peanuts or vinegary olives will clash with most table wines. So buy some proper dry sherry, chill it down and thrill to the world's best aperitif. Fino, manzanilla and amontillado sherries of real quality now feature in all the best supermarkets – some under own labels.

Eggs are supposed to be inimical to wine. Boiled, fried or poached certainly. But an omelette with a glass of wine, of any colour, is surely a match. Salads, especially those with fruit or tomatoes, get the thumbs-down, but I think it's the dressing. Forgo the vinegar, and salad opens up a vinous vista.

Cheese is a conundrum. Red wine goes with cheese, right? But soft cheeses, particularly goat's, can make red wines taste awfully tinny. You're much better off with an exotic and ripe white wine. Sweet white wines make a famously savoury match with blue cheeses. A better match, I believe, than with their conventional companions, puddings. Hard cheeses such as Cheddar may be fine with some red wines, but even better with a glass of Port.

Wine with curry? Now that incendiary dishes are entirely integrated into the national diet, I suppose this is, uh, a burning question. Big, ripe reds such as Australian Shiraz can stand up to Indian heat, and Argentine Malbec seems appropriate for chilli dishes. Chinese cuisine likes aromatic white wines such as Alsace (or New Zealand) Gewürztraminer, and salsa dishes call for zingy dry whites such as Sauvignon Blanc.

But everyone to their own taste. If there's one universal convention in food and wine matching it must surely be to suit yourself.

—A Wine Vocabulary—

A brief guide to the use of language across the wine world – on labels, in literature and among the listings in this book

---
A

AC – *See* Appellation d'Origine Contrôlée.

acidity – Natural acids in grape juice are harnessed by the winemaker to produce clean, crisp flavours. Excess acidity creates rawness or greenness; shortage is indicated by wateriness.

aftertaste – The flavour that lingers in the mouth after swallowing or spitting the wine.

Aglianico – Black grape variety of southern Italy. Vines originally planted by ancient Greek settlers from 600BC in the arid volcanic landscapes of Basilicata and Cilento produce distinctive dark and earthy reds.

Agriculture biologique – On French wine labels, an indication that the wine has been made by organic methods.

Albariño – White grape variety of Spain that makes intriguingly perfumed fresh and tangy dry wines, especially in esteemed Atlantic-facing Rias Baixas region.

alcohol – The alcohol levels in wines are expressed in terms of alcohol by volume ('abv'), that is, the percentage of the volume of the wine that is common, or ethyl, alcohol. A typical wine at 12 per cent abv is thus 12 parts alcohol and, in effect, 88 parts fruit juice. Alcohol is viewed by some health professionals as a poison, but there is actuarial evidence that total abstainers live shorter lives than moderate consumers. The UK Department of Health declares there is no safe level of alcohol consumption, and advises that drinkers should not exceed a weekly number of 'units' of alcohol. A unit is 10ml of pure alcohol, the quantity contained in about half a 175ml glass of wine with 12 per cent alcohol. From 1995, the advisory limit on weekly units was 28 for men and 21 for women. This was reduced in 2016 to 14 for men and women alike.

Alentejo – Wine region of southern Portugal (immediately north of the Algarve), with a fast-improving reputation, especially for sappy, keen reds from local grape varieties including Aragones, Castelão and Trincadeira.

Almansa – DO winemaking region of Spain inland from Alicante, making inexpensive red wines.

Alsace – France's easternmost wine-producing region lies between the Vosges Mountains and the River Rhine, with Germany beyond.

These conditions make for the production of some of the world's most delicious and fascinating white wines, always sold under the name of their constituent grapes. Pinot Blanc is the most affordable – and is well worth looking out for. The 'noble' grape varieties of the region are Gewürztraminer, Muscat, Riesling and Pinot Gris and they are always made on a single-variety basis. The richest, most exotic wines are those from individual *grand cru* vineyards, which are named on the label. Some *vendange tardive* (late harvest) wines are made, and tend to be expensive. All the wines are sold in tall, slim green bottles known as flûtes that closely resemble those of the Mosel. The names of producers as well as grape varieties are often German too, so it is widely assumed that Alsace wines are German in style, if not in nationality. But this is not the case in either particular. Alsace wines are dry and quite unique in character – and definitely French.

amarone – Style of red wine made in Valpolicella, Italy. Specially selected grapes are held back from the harvest and stored for several months to dry them out. They are then pressed and fermented into a highly concentrated speciality dry wine. Amarone means 'bitter', describing the dry style of the flavour.

amontillado – *See* sherry.

aperitif – If a wine is thus described, I believe it will give as much pleasure before a meal as with one. Crisp, low-alcohol German wines and other delicately flavoured whites (including many dry Italians) are examples.

appassimento – Italian technique of drying out new-picked grapes to concentrate the sugars. Varying proportions of appassimento fruit are added to the fermentation of speciality wines such as amarone and ripasso.

Appellation d'Origine Contrôlée – Commonly abbreviated to AC or AOC, this is the system under which top-quality wines have been defined in France since 1935. About a third of the country's vast annual output qualifies across about 500 AC (or AOP – see Appellation d'Origine Protégée) zones. The declaration of an AC on the label signifies that the wine meets standards concerning location of vineyards and wineries, grape varieties and limits on harvest per hectare, methods of cultivation and vinification, and alcohol content. Wines are inspected and tasted by state-appointed committees.

Appellation d'Origine Protégée (AOP) – Under European Union rule changes, the AOC system is gradually transforming into AOP. In effect, it means little more than the exchange of 'controlled' with 'protected' on labels. One quirk of the rules is that makers of AOP wines will be able to name the constituent grape variety or varieties on their labels, if they so wish.

Apulia – Anglicised name for Puglia, Italy.

Aragones – Synonym in Portugal, especially in the Alentejo region, for the Tempranillo grape variety of Spain.

Ardèche – Region of southern France to the west of the Rhône river, home to a good IGP zone including the Coteaux de l'Ardèche. Decent-value reds from Syrah and Cabernet Sauvignon grapes, and less interesting dry whites.

Arneis – White grape variety of Piedmont, north-west Italy. Makes dry whites with a certain almondy richness at often-inflated prices.

Assyrtiko – White grape variety of Greece now commonly named on dry white wines, sometimes of great quality, from the mainland and islands.

Asti – Town and major winemaking centre in Piedmont, Italy. The sparkling (spumante) wines made from Moscato grapes are inexpensive and sweet with a modest 5 to 7 per cent alcohol. Vivid red wine Barbera d'Asti also produced.

attack – In wine-tasting, the first impression made by the wine in the mouth.

Auslese – German wine-quality designation. *See* QmP.

B

Baga – Black grape variety indigenous to Portugal. Makes famously concentrated, juicy reds of deep colour from the grapes' particularly thick skins. Look out for this name, now quite frequently quoted as the varietal on Portuguese wine labels.

balance – A big word in the vocabulary of wine tasting. Respectable wine must get two key things right: lots of fruitiness from the sweet grape juice, and plenty of acidity so the sweetness is 'balanced' with the crispness familiar in good dry whites and the dryness that marks out good reds. Some wines are noticeably 'well balanced' in that they have memorable fruitiness and the clean, satisfying 'finish' (last flavour in the mouth) that ideal acidity imparts.

Barbera – Black grape variety originally of Piedmont in Italy. Most commonly seen as Barbera d'Asti, the vigorously fruity red wine made around Asti – once better known for sweet sparkling Asti Spumante. Barbera grapes are now cultivated in South America, producing less-interesting wine than at home in Italy.

Bardolino – Once fashionable, light red wine DOC of Veneto, north-west Italy. Bardolino is made principally from Corvina Veronese grapes plus Rondinella, Molinara and Negrara. Best wines are supposed to be those labelled Bardolino Superiore, a DOCG created in 2002. This classification closely specifies the permissible grape varieties and sets the alcohol level at a minimum of 12 per cent.

Barossa Valley – Famed vineyard region north of Adelaide, Australia, produces hearty reds principally from Shiraz, Cabernet Sauvignon and Grenache grapes, plus plenty of lush white wine from Chardonnay. Also known for limey, long-lived, mineral dry whites from Riesling grapes.

barrique – Barrel in French. *En barrique* on a wine label signifies the wine has been matured in casks rather than tanks.

Beaujolais – Unique red wines from the southern reaches of Burgundy, France, are made from Gamay grapes. Beaujolais nouveau, now unfashionable, provides a friendly introduction to the bouncy, red-fruit style of the wine, but for the authentic experience, go for Beaujolais Villages, from the region's better, northern vineyards. There are ten AC zones within this northern sector making wines under their own names. Known as the *crus*, these are Brouilly, Chénas, Chiroubles, Côte de Brouilly,

Fleurie, Juliénas, Morgon, Moulin à Vent, Regnié and St Amour. Prices are higher than those for Beaujolais Villages, but not always justifiably so.

Beaumes de Venise – Village near Châteauneuf du Pape in France's Rhône valley, famous for sweet and alcoholic wine from Muscat grapes. Delicious, grapey wines. A small number of growers also make strong (sometimes rather tough) red wines under the village name.

Beaune – One of the two centres (the other is Nuits St Georges) of the Côte d'Or, the winemaking heart of Burgundy in France. Three of the region's humbler appellations take the name of the town: Côtes de Beaune, Côtes de Beaune Villages and Hautes Côtes de Beaune.

berry fruit – Some red wines deliver a burst of flavour in the mouth that corresponds to biting into a newly picked berry – strawberry, blackberry, etc. So a wine described as having berry fruit (by this writer, anyway) has freshness, liveliness and immediate appeal.

bianco – White wine, Italy.

Bical – White grape variety principally of Dão region of northern Portugal. Not usually identified on labels, because most of it goes into inexpensive sparkling wines. Can make still wines of very refreshing crispness.

biodynamics – A cultivation method taking the organic approach several steps further. Biodynamic winemakers plant and tend their vineyards according to a date and time calendar 'in harmony' with the movements of the planets. Some of France's best-known wine estates subscribe, and many more are going that way. It might all sound bonkers, but it's salutary to learn that biodynamics is based on principles first described by the eminent Austrian educationist Rudolph Steiner.

bite – In wine-tasting, the impression on the palate of a wine with plenty of acidity and, often, tannin.

blanc – White wine, France.

blanc de blancs – White wine from white grapes, France. May seem to be stating the obvious, but some white wines (e.g. champagne) are made, partially or entirely, from black grapes.

blanc de noirs – White wine from black grapes, France. Usually sparkling (especially champagne) made from black Pinot Meunier and Pinot Noir grapes, with no Chardonnay or other white varieties.

blanco – White wine, Spain and Portugal.

Blauer Zweigelt – Black grape variety of Austria, making a large proportion of the country's red wines, some of excellent quality.

Bobal – Black grape variety mostly of south-eastern Spain. Thick skin is good for colour and juice contributes acidity to blends.

bodega – In Spain, a wine producer or wine shop.

Bonarda – Black grape variety of northern Italy. Now more widely planted in Argentina, where it makes some well-regarded red wines.

botrytis – Full name, *botrytis cinerea*, is that of a beneficent fungus that can attack ripe grape bunches late in the season, shrivelling the berries to a gruesome-looking mess, which yields concentrated juice of prized sweetness. Cheerfully known as 'noble rot', this fungus is actively encouraged by winemakers in regions as diverse as Sauternes (in Bordeaux),

Monbazillac (in Bergerac), the Rhine and Mosel valleys, Hungary's Tokaji region and South Australia to make ambrosial dessert wines.

bouncy – The feel in the mouth of a red wine with young, juicy fruitiness. Good Beaujolais is bouncy, as are many north-west-Italian wines from Barbera and Dolcetto grapes.

Bourgogne Grand Ordinaire – Former AC of Burgundy, France. *See* Coteaux Bourguignons.

Bourgueil – Appellation of Loire Valley, France. Long-lived red wines from Cabernet Franc grapes.

briary – In wine tasting, associated with the flavours of fruit from prickly bushes such as blackberries.

brûlé – Pleasant burnt-toffee taste or smell, as in crème brûlée.

brut – Driest style of sparkling wine. Originally French, for very dry champagnes specially developed for the British market, but now used for sparkling wines from all round the world.

Buzet – Little-seen AC of south-west France overshadowed by Bordeaux but producing some characterful ripe reds.

C

Cabardès – AC for red and rosé wines from area north of Carcassonne, Aude, France. Principally Cabernet Sauvignon and Merlot grapes.

Cabernet Franc – Black grape variety originally of France. It makes the light-bodied and keenly edged red wines of the Loire Valley – such as Chinon and Saumur. And it is much grown in Bordeaux, especially in the appellation of St Emilion. Also now planted in Argentina, Australia and North America. Wines, especially in the Loire, are characterised by a leafy, sappy style and bold fruitiness. Most are best enjoyed young.

Cabernet Sauvignon – Black (or, rather, blue) grape variety now grown in virtually every wine-producing nation. When perfectly ripened, the grapes are smaller than many other varieties and have particularly thick skins. This means that when pressed, Cabernet grapes have a high proportion of skin to juice – and that makes for wine with lots of colour and tannin. In Bordeaux, the grape's traditional home, the grandest Cabernet-based wines have always been known as *vins de garde* (wines to keep) because they take years, even decades, to evolve as the effect of all that skin extraction preserves the fruit all the way to magnificent maturity. But in today's impatient world, these grapes are exploited in modern winemaking techniques to produce the sublime flavours of mature Cabernet without having to hang around for lengthy periods awaiting maturation. While there's nothing like a fine, ten-year-old claret (and few quite as expensive), there are many excellent Cabernets from around the world that amply illustrate this grape's characteristics. Classic smells and flavours include blackcurrants, cedar wood, chocolate, tobacco – even violets.

Cahors – An AC of the Lot Valley in south-west France once famous for 'black wine'. This was a curious concoction of straightforward wine mixed with a soupy must, made by boiling up new-pressed juice to concentrate it (through evaporation) before fermentation. The myth is still perpetuated that Cahors wine continues to be made in this way, but production on this basis actually ceased 150 years ago. Cahors today is no stronger, or blacker, than the wines of neighbouring appellations. Principal grape variety is Malbec, known locally as Cot.

Cairanne – Village of the appellation collectively known as the Côtes du Rhône in southern France. Cairanne is one of several villages entitled to put their name on the labels of wines made within their AC boundary, and the appearance of this name is quite reliably an indicator of quality.

Calatayud – DO (quality wine zone) near Zaragoza in the Aragon region of northern Spain where they're making some astonishingly good wines at bargain prices, mainly reds from Garnacha and Tempranillo grapes. These are the varieties that go into the polished and oaky wines of Rioja, but in Calatayud, the wines are dark, dense and decidedly different.

Cannonau – Black grape native to Sardinia by name, but in fact the same variety as the ubiquitous Grenache of France (and Garnacha of Spain).

cantina sociale – *See* co-op.

Carignan – Black grape variety of Mediterranean France. It is rarely identified on labels, but is a major constituent of wines from the southern Rhône and Languedoc-Roussillon regions. Known as Carignano in Italy and Cariñena in Spain.

Cariñena – A region of north-east Spain, south of Navarra, known for substantial reds, as well as the Spanish name for the Carignan grape (*qv*).

Carmenère – Black grape variety once widely grown in Bordeaux but abandoned due to cultivation problems. Lately revived in South America where it is producing fine wines, sometimes with echoes of Bordeaux.

cassis – As a tasting note, signifies a wine that has a noticeable blackcurrant-concentrate flavour or smell. Much associated with the Cabernet Sauvignon grape.

Castelao – Portuguese black grape variety. Same as Periquita.

Catarratto – White grape variety of Sicily. In skilled hands it can make anything from keen, green-fruit dry whites to lush, oaked super-ripe styles. Also used for Marsala.

cat's pee – In tasting notes, a jocular reference to the smell of a certain style of Sauvignon Blanc wine.

cava – The sparkling wine of Spain. Most originates in Catalonia, but the Denominación de Origen (DO) guarantee of authenticity is open to producers in many regions of the country. Much cava is very reasonably priced even though it is made by the same method as champagne – second fermentation in bottle, known in Spain as the *método clásico*.

CdR – Côtes du Rhône. My own shorthand.

cépage – Grape variety, French. 'Cépage Merlot' on a label simply means the wine is made largely or exclusively from Merlot grapes.

Chablis – Northernmost AC of France's Burgundy region. Its dry white wines from Chardonnay grapes are known for their fresh and steely style, but the best wines also age very gracefully into complex classics.

Chambourcin – Sounds like a cream cheese but it's a relatively modern (1963) French hybrid black grape that makes some good non-appellation lightweight-but-concentrated reds in the Loire Valley and now some heftier versions in Australia.

champagne – The sparkling wine of the strictly defined Champagne region of France, made by the equally strictly defined champagne method.

Chardonnay – Possibly the world's most popular grape variety. Said to originate from the village of Chardonnay in the Mâconnais region of southern Burgundy, the vine is now planted in every wine-producing nation. Wines are commonly characterised by generous colour and sweet-apple smell, but styles range from lean and sharp to opulently rich. Australia started the craze for oaked Chardonnay, the gold-coloured, super-ripe, buttery 'upfront' wines that are a caricature of lavish and outrageously expensive burgundies such as Meursault and Puligny-Montrachet. Rich to the point of egginess, these Aussie pretenders are now giving way to a sleeker, more minerally style with much less oak presence – if any at all. California and Chile, New Zealand and South Africa are competing hard to imitate the Burgundian style, and Australia's success in doing so.

Châteauneuf du Pape – Famed appellation centred on a picturesque village of the southern Rhône valley in France where in the 1320s French Pope Clement V had a splendid new château built for himself as a summer retreat amidst his vineyards. The red wines of the AC, which can be made from 13 different grape varieties but principally Grenache, Syrah and Mourvèdre, are regarded as the best of the southern Rhône and have become rather expensive – but they can be sensationally good. Expensive white wines are also made.

Chenin Blanc – White grape variety of the Loire Valley, France. Now also grown farther afield, especially in South Africa. Makes dry, soft white wines and also rich, sweet styles.

cherry – In wine tasting, either a pale red colour or, more commonly, a smell or flavour akin to the sun-warmed, bursting sweet ripeness of cherries. Many Italian wines, from lightweights such as Bardolino and Valpolicella to serious Chianti, have this character. 'Black cherry' as a description is often used of Merlot wines – meaning they are sweet but have a firmness of mouthfeel associated with the thicker skins of black cherries.

Cinsault – Black grape variety of southern France, where it is invariably blended with others in wines of all qualities from country reds to pricy appellations such as Châteauneuf du Pape. Also much planted in South Africa. The effect in wine is to add keen aromas (sometimes compared with turpentine) and softness to the blend. The name is often spelt Cinsaut.

Clape, La – A small *cru* (defined quality-vineyard area) within the Coteaux du Languedoc where the growers make some seriously delicious red wines, mainly from Carignan, Grenache and Syrah grapes. A name worth looking out for on labels from the region.

claret – The red wine of Bordeaux, France. Old British nickname from Latin *clarus*, meaning 'clear', recalling a time when the red wines of the region were much lighter in colour than they are now.

clarete – On Spanish labels indicates a pale-coloured red wine. Tinto signifies a deeper hue.

classed growth – English translation of French *cru classé* describes a group of 60 individual wine estates in the Médoc district of Bordeaux, which in 1855 were granted this new status on the basis that their wines were the most expensive of the day. The classification was a promotional wheeze to attract attention to the Bordeaux stand at that year's Great Exhibition in Paris. Amazingly, all of the wines concerned are still in production and most still occupy more or less their original places in the pecking order price-wise. The league was divided up into five divisions from *Premier Grand Cru Classé* (just four wines originally, with one promoted in 1971 – the only change ever made to the classification) to *Cinquième Grand Cru Classé*. Other regions of Bordeaux, notably Graves and St Emilion, have since imitated Médoc and introduced their own rankings of *cru classé* estates.

classic – An overused term in every respect – wine descriptions being no exception. In this book, the word is used to describe a very good wine of its type. So, a 'classic' Cabernet Sauvignon is one that is recognisably and admirably characteristic of that grape.

Classico – Under Italy's wine laws, this word appended to the name of a DOC or DOCG zone has an important significance. The classico wines of the region can only be made from vineyards lying in the best-rated areas, and wines thus labelled (e.g. Chianti Classico, Soave Classico, Valpolicella Classico) can be reliably counted on to be a cut above the rest.

Colombard – White grape variety of southern France. Once employed almost entirely for making the wine that is distilled for armagnac and cognac brandies, but lately restored to varietal prominence in the Côtes de Gascogne where high-tech wineries turn it into a fresh and crisp, if unchallenging, dry wine at a budget price. But beware, cheap Colombard (especially from South Africa) can still be very dull.

Conca de Barbera – Winemaking region of Catalonia, Spain.

co-op – Very many of France's good-quality, inexpensive wines are made by co-operatives. These are wine-producing centres whose members, and joint-owners, are local *vignerons* (vine growers). Each year they sell their harvests to the co-op for turning into branded wines. In Italy, co-op wines can be identified by the words *Cantina Sociale* on the label and in Germany by the term *Winzergenossenschaft*.

Corbières – A name to look out for. It's an AC of France's Midi (deep south) and produces countless robust reds and a few interesting whites, often at bargain prices.

Cortese – White grape variety of Piedmont, Italy. At its best, makes delicious, keenly brisk and fascinating wines, including those of the Gavi DOCG. Worth seeking out.

Costières de Nîmes – Until 1989, this AC of southern France was known as the Costières de Gard. It forms a buffer between the southern Rhône and Languedoc-Roussillon regions, and makes wines from broadly the same range of grape varieties. It's a name to look out for, the best red wines being notable for their concentration of colour and fruit, with the earthy-spiciness of the better Rhône wines and a likeable liquorice note. A few good white wines, too, and even a decent rosé or two.

Côte – In French, it simply means a side, or slope, of a hill. The implication in wine terms is that the grapes come from a vineyard ideally situated for maximum sunlight, good drainage and the unique soil conditions prevailing on the hill in question. It's fair enough to claim that vines grown on slopes might get more sunlight than those grown on the flat, but there is no guarantee whatsoever that any wine labelled 'Côtes du' this or that is made from grapes grown on a hillside anyway. Côtes du Rhône wines are a case in point. Many 'Côtes' wines come from entirely level vineyards and it is worth remembering that many of the vineyards of Bordeaux, producing most of the world's priciest wines, are little short of prairie-flat. The quality factor is determined much more significantly by the weather and the talents of the winemaker.

Coteaux Bourguignons – Generic AC of Burgundy, France, since 2011 for red and rosé wines from Pinot Noir and Gamay grapes, and white wines from (principally) Chardonnay and Bourgogne Aligoté grapes. The AC replaces the former appellation Bourgogne Grand Ordinaire.

Côtes de Blaye – Appellation Contrôlée zone of Bordeaux on the right bank of the River Gironde, opposite the more prestigious Médoc zone of the left bank. Best-rated vineyards qualify for the AC Premières Côtes de Blaye. A couple of centuries ago, Blaye (pronounced 'bligh') was the grander of the two, and even today makes some wines that compete well for quality, and at a fraction of the price of wines from its more fashionable rival across the water.

Côtes de Bourg – AC neighbouring Côtes de Blaye, making red wines of decent quality and value.

Côtes du Luberon – Appellation Contrôlée zone of Provence in south-east France. Wines, mostly red, are similar in style to Côtes du Rhône.

Côtes du Rhône – One of the biggest and best-known appellations of south-east France, covering an area roughly defined by the southern reaches of the valley of the River Rhône. The Côtes du Rhône AC achieves notably consistent quality at all points along the price scale. Lots of brilliant-value warm and spicy reds, principally from Grenache and Syrah grapes. There are also some white and rosé wines.

Côtes du Rhône Villages – Appellation within the larger Côtes du Rhône AC for wine of supposed superiority made in a number of zones associated with a long list of nominated individual villages.

Côtes du Roussillon – Huge appellation of south-west France known for strong, dark, peppery reds often offering very decent value.

Côtes du Roussillon Villages – Appellation for superior wines from a number of nominated locations within the larger Roussillon AC. Some of these village wines can be of exceptional quality and value.

crianza – Means 'nursery' in Spanish. On Rioja and Navarra wines, the designation signifies a wine that has been nursed through a maturing period of at least a year in oak casks and a further six months in bottle before being released for sale.

cru – A word that crops up with confusing regularity on French wine labels. It means 'the growing' or 'the making' of a wine and asserts that the wine concerned is from a specific vineyard. Under the Appellation Contrôlée rules, countless *crus* are classified in various hierarchical ranks. Hundreds of individual vineyards are described as *premier cru* or *grand cru* in the classic wine regions of Alsace, Bordeaux, Burgundy and Champagne. The common denominator is that the wine can be counted on to be expensive. On humbler wines, the use of the word *cru* tends to be mere decoration.

cru classé – *See* classed growth.

cuve – A vat for wine. French.

cuvée – French for the wine in a *cuve*, or vat. The word is much used on labels to imply that the wine is from just one vat, and thus of unique, unblended character. *Première cuvée* is supposedly the best wine from a given pressing because it comes from the free-run juice of grapes crushed by their own weight before pressing begins. Subsequent *cuvées* will have been from harsher pressings, grinding the grape pulp to extract the last drops of juice.

D

Dão – Major wine-producing region of northern Portugal now turning out much more interesting reds than it used to – worth looking out for anything made by mega-producer Sogrape.

demi sec – 'Half-dry' style of French (and some other) wines. Beware. It can mean anything from off-dry to cloyingly sweet.

DO – Denominación de Origen, Spain's wine-regulating scheme, similar to France's AC, but older – the first DO region was Rioja, from 1926. DO wines are Spain's best, accounting for a third of the nation's annual production.

DOC – Stands for Denominazione di Origine Controllata, Italy's equivalent of France's AC. The wines are made according to the stipulations of each of the system's 300-plus denominated zones of origin, along with a further 74 zones, which enjoy the superior classification of DOCG (DOC with *e Garantita* – guaranteed – appended).

DOCa – *Denominación de Origen Calificada* is Spain's highest regional wine classification; currently only Priorat and Rioja qualify.

DOP – Denominazione di Origine Protetta is an alternative classification to DOC (*qv*) under EU directive in Italy, comparable to AOP (*qv*) in France, but not yet widely adopted.

Durif – Rare black grape variety mostly of California, where it is also known as Petite Sirah, with some plantings in Australia.

E

earthy – A tricky word in the wine vocabulary. In this book, its use is meant to be complimentary. It indicates that the wine somehow suggests the soil the grapes were grown in, even (perhaps a shade too poetically) the landscape in which the vineyards lie. The amazing-value red wines of the torrid, volcanic southernmost regions of Italy are often described as earthy. This is an association with the pleasantly 'scorched' back-flavour in wines made from the ultra-ripe harvests of this near-sub-tropical part of the world.

edge – A wine with edge is one with evident (although not excessive) acidity.

élevé – 'Brought up' in French. Much used on wine labels where the wine has been matured (brought up) in oak barrels, *élevé en fûts de chêne*, to give it extra dimensions.

Entre Deux Mers – Meaning 'between two seas', it's a region lying between the Dordogne and Garonne rivers of Bordeaux, now mainly known for dry white wines from Sauvignon Blanc and Semillon grapes.

Estremadura – Wine-producing region occupying Portugal's coastal area north of Lisbon. Lots of interesting wines from indigenous grape varieties, often at bargain prices. If a label mentions Estremadura, it is a safe rule that there might be something good within.

Extremadura – Minor wine-producing region of western Spain abutting the frontier with Portugal's Alentejo region. Not to be confused with Estremadura of Portugal (above).

F

Falanghina – Revived ancient grape variety of southern Italy now making some superbly fresh and tangy white wines.

Faugères – AC of the Languedoc in south-west France. Source of many hearty, economic reds.

Feteasca – White grape variety widely grown in Romania. Name means 'maiden's grape' and the wine tends to be soft and slightly sweet.

Fiano – White grape variety of the Campania of southern Italy and Sicily, lately revived. It is said to have been cultivated by the ancient Romans for a wine called Apianum.

finish – The last flavour lingering in the mouth after wine has been swallowed.

fino – Pale and very dry style of sherry. You drink it thoroughly chilled – and you don't keep it any longer after opening than other dry white wines. Needs to be fresh to be at its best.

Fitou – AC of Languedoc, France. Red wines principally from Carignan, Grenache, Mourvèdre and Syrah grapes.

flabby – Fun word describing a wine that tastes dilute or watery, with insufficient acidity.

Frappato – Black grape variety of Sicily. Light red wines.

fruit – In tasting terms, the fruit is the greater part of the overall flavour of a wine. The wine is, after all, composed entirely of fruit

G

Gamay – The black grape that makes all red Beaujolais and some ordinary burgundy. It is a pretty safe rule to avoid Gamay wines from other regions.

Garganega – White grape variety of the Veneto region of north-east Italy. Best known as the principal ingredient of Soave, but occasionally included in varietal blends and mentioned as such on labels. Correctly pronounced 'gar-GAN-iga'.

Garnacha – Spanish black grape variety synonymous with Grenache of France. It is blended with Tempranillo to make the red wines of Rioja and Navarra, and is now quite widely cultivated elsewhere in Spain to make grippingly fruity varietals.

garrigue – Arid land of France's deep south giving its name to a style of red wine that notionally evokes the herby, heated, peppery flavours associated with such a landscape and its flora. A tricky metaphor.

Gavi – DOCG for dry aromatic white wine from Cortese grapes in Piedmont, north-west Italy. Trendy Gavi di Gavi wines tend to be enjoyably lush, but are rather expensive.

Gewürztraminer – One of the great grape varieties of Alsace, France. At their best, the wines are perfumed with lychees and are richly, spicily fruity, yet quite dry. Gewürztraminer from Alsace can be expensive, but the grape is also grown with some success in Germany, Italy, New Zealand and South America, at more approachable prices. Pronounced 'ge-VOORTS-traminner'.

Givry – AC for red and white wines in the Côte Chalonnaise sub-region of Burgundy. Source of some wonderfully natural-tasting reds that might be lighter than those of the more prestigious Côte d'Or to the north, but have great merits of their own. Relatively, the wines are often underpriced.

Glera – New official name for the Prosecco grape of northern Italy.

Godello – White grape variety of Galicia, Spain.

Graciano – Black grape variety of Spain that is one of the minor constituents of Rioja. Better known in its own right in Australia where it can make dense, spicy, long-lived red wines.

green – I don't often use this in the pejorative. Green, to me, is a likeable degree of freshness, especially in Sauvignon Blanc wines.

Grecanico – White grape variety of southern Italy, especially Sicily. Aromatic, grassy dry white wines.

Greco – White grape variety of southern Italy believed to be of ancient Greek origin. Big-flavoured dry white wines.

Grenache – The mainstay of the wines of the southern Rhône Valley in France. Grenache is usually the greater part of the mix in Côtes du Rhône reds and is widely planted right across the neighbouring Languedoc-Roussillon region. It's a big-cropping variety that thrives even in the hottest climates and is really a blending grape – most commonly with Syrah, the noble variety of the northern Rhône. Few French wines are labelled with its name, but the grape has caught on in Australia in a big way and it is now becoming a familiar varietal, known for strong, dark liquorous reds. Grenache is the French name for what is originally a Spanish variety, Garnacha.

Grillo – White grape of Sicily said to be among the island's oldest indigenous varieties, pre-dating the arrival of the Greeks in 600 BC. Much used for fortified Marsala, it has lately been revived for interesting, aromatic dry table wines.

grip – In wine-tasting terminology, the sensation in the mouth produced by a wine that has a healthy quantity of tannin in it. A wine with grip is a good wine. A wine with too much tannin, or which is still too young (the tannin hasn't 'softened' with age) is not described as having grip, but as mouth-puckering – or simply undrinkable.

Grolleau – Black grape variety of the Loire Valley principally cultivated for Rosé d'Anjou.

Gros Plant – White grape variety of the Pays Nantais in France's Loire estuary; synonymous with the Folle Blanche grape of south-west France.

Grüner Veltliner – The 'national' white-wine grape of Austria. In the past it made mostly soft, German-style everyday wines, but now is behind some excellent dry styles, too.

H

halbtrocken – 'Half-dry' in Germany's wine vocabulary. A reassurance that the wine is not a sugared Liebfraumilch-style confection.

hard – In red wine, a flavour denoting excess tannin, probably due to immaturity.

Haut-Médoc – Extensive AC of Bordeaux accounting for the greater part of the vineyard area to the north of the city of Bordeaux west of the Gironde river. The Haut-Médoc incorporates the prestigious commune-ACs of Listrac, Margaux, Moulis, Pauillac, St Estèphe and St Julien.

Hermitage – AC of northern Rhône Valley, France for red wines from Syrah grapes and some whites. Hermitage is also the regional name in South Africa for the Cinsaut grape.

hock – The wine of Germany's Rhine river valleys. Traditionally, but no longer consistently, it comes in brown bottles, as distinct from the wine of the Mosel river valleys – which comes in green ones.

Hunter Valley – Long-established (1820s) wine-producing region of New South Wales, Australia.

I

Indicación Geográfica Protegida (IGP) – Spain's country-wine quality designation covers 46 zones across the country. Wines made under the IGP can be labelled Vino de la Tierra.

Indication Géographique Protégée (IGP) – Introduced to France in 2010 under EU-wide wine-designation rules, IGP covers the wines previously known as vins de pays. Some wines are currently labelled IGP, but established vins de pays producers are redesignating slowly, if at all, and are not obliged to do so. Some will abbreviate, so, for example, Vin de Pays d'Oc shortens to Pays d'Oc.

Indicazione Geografica Tipica (IGT) – Italian wine-quality designation, broadly equivalent to France's IGP. The label has to state the geographical location of the vineyard and will often (but not always) state the principal grape varieties from which the wine is made.

isinglass – A gelatinous material used in fining (clarifying) wine. It is derived from fish bladders and consequently is eschewed by makers of 'vegetarian' or 'vegan' wines.

J

jammy – The 'sweetness' in dry red wines is supposed to evoke ripeness rather than sugariness. Sometimes, flavours include a sweetness reminiscent of jam. Usually a fault in the winemaking technique.

Jerez – Wine town of Andalucia, Spain, and home to sherry. The English word 'sherry' is a simple mispronunciation of Jerez.

joven – Young wine, Spanish. In regions such as Rioja, *vino joven* is a synonym for *sin crianza*, which means 'without ageing' in cask or bottle.

Jura – Wine region of eastern France incorporating four AOCs, Arbois, Château-Chalon, Côtes du Jura and L'Etoile. Known for still red, white and rosé wines and sparkling wines as well as exotic *vin de paille* and *vin jaune*.

Jurançon – Appellation for white wines from Courbu and Manseng grapes at Pau, south-west France.

K

Kabinett – Under Germany's bewildering wine-quality rules, this is a classification of a top-quality (QmP) wine. Expect a keen, dry, racy style. The name comes from the cabinet or cupboard in which winemakers traditionally kept their most treasured bottles.

Kekfrankos – Black grape variety of Hungary, particularly the Sopron region, which makes some of the country's more interesting red wines, characterised by colour and spiciness. Same variety as Austria's Blaufrankisch.

L

Ladoix – Unfashionable AC at northern edge of Côtes de Beaune makes some of Burgundy's true bargain reds. A name to look out for.

Lambrusco – The name is that of a black grape variety widely grown across northern Italy. True Lambrusco wine is red, dry and very slightly sparkling, and enjoying a current vogue in Britain.

Languedoc-Roussillon – Extensive wine region of southern France incorporating numerous ACs and IGP zones, notably the Pays d'Oc and Côtes de Roussillon.

lees – The detritus of the winemaking process that collects in the bottom of the vat or cask. Wines left for extended periods on the lees can acquire extra dimensions of flavour, in particular a 'leesy' creaminess.

legs – The liquid residue left clinging to the sides of the glass after wine has been swirled. The persistence of the legs is an indicator of the weight of alcohol. Also known as 'tears'.

lieu dit – This is starting to appear on French wine labels. It translates as an 'agreed place' and is an area of vineyard defined as of particular character or merit, but not classified under wine law. Usually, the *lieu dit*'s name is stated, with the implication that the wine in question has special merit.

liquorice – The pungent, slightly burnt flavours of this confection are detectable in some wines made from very ripe grapes, for example, the Malbec harvested in Argentina and several varieties grown in the very hot vineyards of southernmost Italy. A close synonym is 'tarry'. This characteristic is by no means a fault in red wine, unless very dominant, but it can make for a challenging flavour that might not appeal to all tastes.

liquorous – Wines of great weight and glyceriney texture (evidenced by the 'legs', or 'tears', which cling to the glass after the wine has been swirled) are always noteworthy. The connection with liquor is drawn in respect of the feel of the wine in the mouth, rather than with the higher alcoholic strength of spirits.

Lirac – Village and AC of southern Rhône Valley, France. A near-neighbour of the esteemed appellation of Châteauneuf du Pape, Lirac makes red wine of comparable depth and complexity, at competitive prices.

Lugana – DOC of Lombardy, Italy, known for a dry white wine that is often of real distinction – rich, almondy stuff from the ubiquitous Trebbiano grape.

M

Macabeo – One of the main grapes used for cava, the sparkling wine of Spain. It is the same grape as Viura.

Mâcon – Town and collective appellation of southern Burgundy, France. Minerally white wines from Chardonnay grapes and light reds from Pinot Noir and some Gamay. The better ones, and the ones exported, have the AC Mâcon-Villages and there are individual village wines with their own ACs including Mâcon-Clessé, Mâcon-Viré and Mâcon-Lugny.

Malbec – Black grape variety grown on a small scale in Bordeaux, and the mainstay of the wines of Cahors in France's Dordogne region under the name Cot. Now much better known for producing big butch reds in Argentina.

malolactic fermentation – In winemaking, a common natural bacterial action following alcoholic fermentation, converting malic (apple) acid into lactic (milk) acid. The effect is to reduce tartness and to boost creaminess in the wine. Adding lactic bacteria to wine to promote the process is widely practised.

manzanilla – Pale, very dry sherry of Sanlucar de Barrameda, a resort town on the Bay of Cadiz in Spain. Manzanilla is proud to be distinct from the pale, very dry fino sherry of the main producing town of Jerez de la Frontera an hour's drive inland. Drink it chilled and fresh – it goes downhill in an opened bottle after just a few days, even if kept (as it should be) in the fridge.

Margaret River – Vineyard region of Western Australia regarded as ideal for grape varieties including Cabernet Sauvignon. It has a relatively cool climate and a reputation for making sophisticated wines, both red and white.

Marlborough – Best-known vineyard region of New Zealand's South Island has a cool climate and a name for brisk but cerebral Sauvignon Blanc and Chardonnay wines.

Marsanne – White grape variety of the northern Rhône Valley and, increasingly, of the wider south of France. It's known for making well-coloured wines with heady aroma and nuanced fruit.

Mataro – Black grape variety of Australia. It's the same as the Mourvèdre of France and Monastrell of Spain.

Mazuelo – Spanish name for France's black grape variety Carignan.

McLaren Vale – Vineyard region south of Adelaide in south-east Australia. Known for blockbuster Shiraz (and Chardonnay) that can be of great balance and quality from winemakers who manage to keep the ripeness under control.

meaty – In wine-tasting, a weighty, rich red wine style.

Mencia – Black grape variety of Galicia and north-west Spain. Light red wines.

Mendoza – Wine region of Argentina. Lying to the east of the Andes mountains, just about opposite the best vineyards of Chile on the other side, Mendoza accounts for the bulk of Argentine wine production.

Merlot – One of the great black wine grapes of Bordeaux, and now grown all over the world. The name is said to derive from the French *merle*, a blackbird. Characteristics of Merlot-based wines attract descriptions such as 'plummy' and 'plump' with black-cherry aromas. The grapes are larger than most, and thus have less skin in proportion to their flesh. This means the resulting wines have less tannin than wines from smaller-berry varieties such as Cabernet Sauvignon, and are therefore, in the Bordeaux context at least, more suitable for drinking while still relatively young.

middle palate – In wine-tasting, the impression given by the wine after the first impact on 'entry' and before the 'finish' when the wine is swallowed.

Midi – Catch-all term for the deep south of France west of the Rhône Valley.

mineral – Irresistible term in wine-tasting. To me it evokes flavours such as the stone-pure freshness of some Loire dry whites, or the flinty quality of the more austere style of the Chardonnay grape, especially in Chablis. Mineral really just means something mined, as in dug out of the ground, like iron ore (as in 'steely' whites) or rock, as in, er, stone. Maybe there's something in it, but I am not entirely confident.

Minervois – AC for (mostly) red wines from vineyards around the Roman-founded town of Minerve in the Languedoc-Roussillon region of France. Often good value. The recently elevated Minervois La Livinière AC is a sort of Minervois *grand cru*.

Monastrell – Black grape variety of Spain, widely planted in Mediterranean regions for inexpensive wines notable for their high alcohol and toughness – though they can mature into excellent, soft reds. The variety is known in France as Mourvèdre and in Australia as Mataro.

Monbazillac – AC for sweet, dessert wines within the wider appellation of Bergerac in south-west France. Made from the same grape varieties (principally Sauvignon and Semillon) that go into the much costlier counterpart wines of Barsac and Sauternes near Bordeaux, these stickies from botrytis-affected, late-harvested grapes can be delicious and good value for money.

Montalcino – Hill town of Tuscany, Italy, and a DOCG for strong and very long-lived red wines from Brunello grapes. The wines are mostly very expensive. Rosso di Montalcino, a DOC for the humbler wines of the zone, is often a good buy.

Montepulciano – Black grape variety of Italy. Best known in Montepulciano d'Abruzzo, the juicy, purply-black and bramble-fruited red of the Abruzzi region midway down Italy's Adriatic side. Also the grape in the rightly popular hearty reds of Rosso Conero from around Ancona in the Marches. Not to be confused with the hill town of Montepulciano in Tuscany, famous for expensive Vino Nobile di Montepulciano wine, made from Sangiovese grapes.

morello – Lots of red wines have smells and flavours redolent of cherries. Morello cherries, among the darkest coloured and sweetest of all varieties and the preferred choice of cherry-brandy producers, have a distinct sweetness resembled by some wines made from Merlot grapes. A morello whiff or taste is generally very welcome.

Moscatel – Spanish Muscat.

Moscato – *See* Muscat.

moselle – The wine of Germany's Mosel river valleys, collectively known for winemaking purposes as the Mosel-Saar-Ruwer. The wine always comes in slim, green bottles, as distinct from the brown bottles traditionally, but no longer exclusively, employed for Rhine wines.

Mourvèdre – Widely planted black grape variety of southern France. It's an ingredient in many of the wines of Provence, the Rhône and Languedoc, including the ubiquitous Pays d'Oc. It's a hot-climate vine and the wine is usually blended with other varieties to give sweet aromas and 'backbone' to the mix. Known as Mataro in Australia and Monastrell in Spain.

Muscadet – One of France's most familiar everyday whites, made from a grape called the Melon or Melon de Bourgogne. It comes from vineyards at the estuarial end of the River Loire, and has a sea-breezy freshness about it. The better wines are reckoned to be those from the vineyards in the Sèvre et Maine region, and many are made *sur lie* – 'on the lees' – meaning that the wine is left in contact with the yeasty deposit of its fermentation until just before bottling, in an endeavour to add interest to what can sometimes be an acidic and fruitless style.

Muscat – Grape variety with origins in ancient Greece, and still grown widely among the Aegean islands for the production of sweet white wines. Muscats are the wines that taste more like grape juice than any other – but the high sugar levels ensure they are also among the most alcoholic of wines, too. Known as Moscato in Italy, the grape is much used for making sweet sparkling wines, as in Asti Spumante or Moscato d'Asti. There are several appellations in south-west France for inexpensive Muscats made rather like port, part-fermented before the addition of grape alcohol to halt the conversion of sugar into alcohol, creating a sweet and heady *vin doux naturel*. Dry Muscat wines, when well made, have a delicious sweet aroma but a refreshing, light touch with flavours reminiscent variously of orange blossom, wood smoke and grapefruit.

must – New-pressed grape juice prior to fermentation.

N

Navarra – DO wine-producing region of northern Spain adjacent to, and overshadowed by, Rioja. Navarra's wines can be startlingly akin to their neighbouring rivals, and sometimes rather better value for money.

négociant – In France, a dealer-producer who buys wines from growers and matures and/or blends them for bottling and sale under his or her own label. Purists can be a bit sniffy about these entrepreneurs, claiming that only the vine-grower with his or her own winemaking set-up can make truly authentic stuff, but the truth is that many of the best wines of France are *négociant*-produced – especially at the humbler end of the price scale. *Négociants* are often identified on wine labels as *négociant-éleveur* (literally 'dealer-bringer-up'), meaning that the wine has been matured, blended and bottled by the party in question.

Negroamaro – Black grape variety mainly of Puglia, the much-lauded wine region of south-east Italy. Dense, earthy red wines with ageing potential and plenty of alcohol. The name is probably (if not obviously) derived from Italian *negro* (black) and *amaro* (bitter). The grape behind Copertino, Salice Salentino and Squinzano.

Nerello Mascalese – Black grape of Sicily, most prolific in vineyards surrounding Mount Etna, making distinctive, flavoursome reds.

Nero d'Avola – Black grape variety of Sicily (Avola is a town in the province of Syracuse) and southern Italy. It makes deep-coloured wines that, given half a chance, can develop intensity and richness with age.

non-vintage – A wine is described as such when it has been blended from the harvests of more than one year. A non-vintage wine is not necessarily an inferior one, but under quality-control regulations around the world, still table wines most usually derive solely from one year's grape crop to qualify for appellation status. Champagnes and sparkling wines are mostly blended from several vintages, as are fortified wines such as port and sherry.

nose – In the vocabulary of the wine-taster, the nose is the scent of a wine. Sounds a bit dotty, but it makes a sensible enough alternative to the rather bald 'smell'. The use of the word 'perfume' implies that the wine smells particularly good. 'Aroma' is used specifically to describe a wine that smells as it should, as in 'this burgundy has the authentic strawberry-raspberry aroma of Pinot Noir'.

O

oak – Most of the world's costliest wines are matured in new or nearly new oak barrels, giving additional opulence of flavour. Of late, many cheaper wines have been getting the oak treatment, too, in older, cheaper casks, or simply by having sacks of oak chippings poured into their steel or fibreglass holding tanks. 'Oak aged' on a label is likely to indicate the latter treatments. But the overtly oaked wines of Australia have in some cases been so overdone that there is now a reactive trend whereby some producers proclaim their wines – particularly Chardonnays – as 'unoaked' on the label, thereby asserting that the flavours are more naturally achieved.

Oltrepo Pavese – Wine-producing zone of Piedmont, north-west Italy. The name means 'south of Pavia across the [river] Po' and the wines, both white and red, can be excellent quality and value for money.

organic wine – As in other sectors of the food industry, demand for organically made wine is – or appears to be – growing. As a rule, a wine qualifies as organic if it comes entirely from grapes grown in vineyards cultivated without the use of synthetic materials, and made in a winery where chemical treatments or additives are shunned with similar vigour. In fact, there are plenty of winemakers in the world using organic methods, but who disdain to label their bottles as such. Wines proclaiming their organic status used to carry the same sort of premium as their counterparts round the corner in the fruit, vegetable and meat aisles. But organic viticulture is now commonplace and there seems little price impact. There is no single worldwide (or even Europe-wide) standard for organic food or wine, so you pretty much have to take the producer's word for it.

P

Pasqua – One of the biggest and, it should be said, best wine producers of the Veneto region of north-west Italy.

Passerina – White grape variety of Marche, Italy. Used in blending but there is also a regional Passerina DOC.

Passetoutgrains – Designation for wine made from more than one grape variety grown in the same vineyard. French. Mostly red burgundy from Gamay and Pinot Noir.

Pays d'Oc – Shortened form under recent rule changes of French wine designation Vin de Pays d'Oc. All other similar regional designations can be similarly abbreviated.

Pecorino – White grape variety of mid-eastern Italy currently in vogue for well-coloured dry white varietal wines.

Periquita – Black grape variety of southern Portugal. Makes rather exotic spicy reds. Name means 'parrot'.

Perricone – Black grape variety of Sicily. Low-acid red wines.

PET – It's what they call plastic wine bottles – lighter to transport and allegedly as ecological as glass. Polyethylene terephthalate.

Petit Verdot – Black grape variety of Bordeaux contributing additional colour, density and spiciness to Cabernet Sauvignon-dominated blends. Mostly a minority player at home, but in Australia and California it is grown as the principal variety for some big hearty reds of real character.

petrol – When white wines from certain grapes, especially Riesling, are allowed to age in the bottle for longer than a year or two, they can take on a spirity aroma reminiscent of petrol or diesel. In grand mature German wines, this is considered a good thing.

Picpoul – Grape variety of southern France. Best known in Picpoul de Pinet, a dry white from near Sète on the Golfe de Lyon, lately elevated to AOP status. The name Picpoul (also Piquepoul) means 'stings the lips' – referring to the natural high acidity of the juice.

Piemonte – North-western province of Italy, which we call Piedmont, known for the spumante wines of the town of Asti, plus expensive Barbaresco and Barolo and better-value varietal red wines from Nebbiolo, Barbera and Dolcetto grapes.

Pinotage – South Africa's own black grape variety. Makes red wines ranging from light and juicy to dark, strong and long-lived. It's a cross between Pinot Noir and a grape the South Africans used to call Hermitage (thus the portmanteau name) but turns out to have been Cinsault.

Pinot Blanc – White grape variety principally of Alsace, France. Florally perfumed, exotically fruity dry white wines.

Pinot Grigio – White grape variety of northern Italy. Wines bearing its name are perplexingly fashionable. Good examples have an interesting smoky-pungent aroma and keen, slaking fruit. But most are dull. Originally French, it is at its best in the lushly exotic Pinot Gris wines of Alsace and is also successfully cultivated in Germany and New Zealand.

Pinot Noir – The great black grape of Burgundy, France. It makes all the region's fabulously expensive red wines. Notoriously difficult to grow in warmer climates, it is nevertheless cultivated by countless intrepid winemakers in the New World intent on reproducing the magic appeal of red burgundy. California and New Zealand have come closest. Some Chilean Pinot Noirs are inexpensive and worth trying.

Pouilly Fuissé – Village and AC of the Mâconnais region of southern Burgundy in France. Dry white wines from Chardonnay grapes. Wines are among the highest rated of the Mâconnais.

Pouilly Fumé – Village and AC of the Loire Valley in France. Dry white wines from Sauvignon Blanc grapes. Similar 'pebbly', 'grassy' or 'gooseberry' style to neighbouring AC Sancerre. The notion put about by some enthusiasts that Pouilly Fumé is 'smoky' is surely nothing more than word association with the name.

Primitivo – Black grape variety of southern Italy, especially the region of Puglia. Named from Latin *primus* for first, the grape is among the earliest-ripening of all varieties. The wines are typically dense and dark in colour with plenty of alcohol, and have an earthy, spicy style.

Priorat – Emerging wine region of Catalonia, Spain. Highly valued red wines from Garnacha and other varieties. Generic brands available in supermarkets are well worth trying out.

Prosecco – Softly sparkling wine of Italy's Veneto region. The best come from the DOCG Conegliano-Valdobbiadene, made as spumante ('foaming') wines in pressurised tanks, typically to 11 per cent alcohol and ranging from softly sweet to crisply dry. The constituent grape, previously also known as Prosecco, has been officially assigned the name Glera.

Puglia – The region occupying the 'heel' of southern Italy, making many good, inexpensive wines from indigenous grape varieties.

QbA – German, standing for Qualitätswein bestimmter Anbaugebiete. It means 'quality wine from designated areas' and implies that the wine is made from grapes with a minimum level of ripeness, but it's by no means a guarantee of exciting quality. Only wines labelled QmP (see next entry) can be depended upon to be special.

QmP – Stands for Qualitätswein mit Prädikat. These are the serious wines of Germany, made without the addition of sugar to 'improve' them. To qualify for QmP status, the grapes must reach a level of ripeness as measured on a sweetness scale – all according to Germany's fiendishly complicated wine-quality regulations. Wines from grapes that reach the stated minimum level of sweetness qualify for the description of Kabinett. The next level up earns the rank of Spätlese, meaning 'late-picked'. Kabinett wines can be expected to be dry and brisk in style, and Spätlese wines a little bit riper and fuller. The next grade up, Auslese, meaning 'selected harvest', indicates a wine made from super-ripe grapes; it will be golden in colour and honeyed in flavour. A generation ago, these wines were as valued, and as expensive, as any of the world's grandest appellations. Beerenauslese and Trockenbeerenauslese are speciality wines made from individually picked late-harvest grapes.

Quincy – AC of Loire Valley, France, known for pebbly-dry white wines from Sauvignon grapes. The wines are forever compared to those of nearby and much better-known Sancerre – and Quincy often represents better value for money. Pronounced 'KAN-see'.

Quinta – Portuguese for farm or estate. It precedes the names of many of Portugal's best-known wines. It is pronounced 'KEEN-ta'.

R

racy – Evocative wine-tasting description for wine that thrills the tastebuds with a rush of exciting sensations. Good Rieslings often qualify.

raisiny – Wines from grapes that have been very ripe or overripe at harvest can take on a smell and flavour akin to the concentrated, heat-dried sweetness of raisins. As a minor element in the character of a wine, this can add to the appeal but as a dominant characteristic it is a fault.

rancio – Spanish term harking back to Roman times when wines were commonly stored in jars outside, exposed to the sun, so they oxidised and took on a burnt sort of flavour. Today, *rancio* describes a baked – and by no means unpleasant – flavour in fortified wines, particularly sherry and Madeira.

Reserva – In Portugal and Spain, this has genuine significance. The Portuguese use it for special wines with a higher alcohol level and longer ageing, although the precise periods vary between regions. In Spain, especially in the Navarra and Rioja regions, it means the wine must have had at least a year in oak and two in bottle before release.

reserve – On French (as *réserve*) or other wines, this implies special-quality, longer-aged wines, but has no official significance.

residual sugar – There is sugar in all wine, left over from the fermentation process. Some producers now mention the quantity of residual sugar on back labels in grams per litre of wine, even though so far there is no legal obligation to do so. Dry wines, red or white, typically have 3 g/l or fewer. Above that, you might well be able to taste the sweetness. In southern hemisphere wines, made from grapes that have ripened under more-intense sunlight than their European counterparts, sugar levels can be correspondingly higher. Sweet wines such as Sauternes contain up to 150 g/l. Dry ('brut') sparkling wines made by the 'champagne' method typically have 10 g/l and tank-method fizzes such as prosecco up to 15 g/l.

Retsina – The universal white wine of Greece. It has been traditionally made in Attica, the region of Athens, for a very long time, and is said to owe its origins and name to the ancient custom of sealing amphorae (terracotta jars) of the wine with a gum made from pine resin. Some of the flavour of the resin inevitably transmitted itself into the wine, and ancient Greeks acquired a lasting taste for it.

Reuilly – AC of Loire Valley, France, for crisp dry whites from Sauvignon grapes. Pronounced 'RER-yee'.

Ribatejo – Emerging wine region of Portugal. Worth seeking out on labels of red wines in particular, because new winemakers are producing lively stuff from distinctive indigenous grapes such as Castelao and Trincadeira.

Ribera del Duero – Classic wine region of north-west Spain lying along the River Duero (which crosses the border to become Portugal's Douro, forming the valley where port comes from). It is home to an estate oddly named Vega Sicilia, where red wines of epic quality are made and sold at equally epic prices. Further down the scale, some very good reds are made, too.

Riesling – The noble grape variety of Germany. It is correctly pronounced 'REEZ-ling', not 'RICE-ling'. Once notorious as the grape behind all those boring 'medium' Liebfraumilches and Niersteiners, this grape has had a bad press. In fact, there has never been much, if any, Riesling in German plonk. But the country's best wines, the so-called Qualitätswein mit Prädikat grades, are made almost exclusively with Riesling. These wines range from crisply fresh and appley styles to extravagantly fruity, honeyed wines from late-harvested grapes. Excellent Riesling wines are also made in Alsace and now in Australasia.

Rioja – The principal fine-wine region of Spain, in the country's north east. The pricier wines are noted for their vanilla-pod richness from long ageing in oak casks. Tempranillo and Garnacha grapes make the reds, Viura the whites.

Ripasso – A particular style of Valpolicella wine. New wine is partially refermented in vats that have been used to make Recioto reds (wines made from semi-dried grapes), thus creating a bigger, smoother version of usually light and pale Valpolicella.

Riserva – In Italy, a wine made only in the best vintages, and allowed longer ageing in cask and bottle.

Rivaner – Alternative name for Germany's Müller-Thurgau grape.

Riverland – Vineyard region to the immediate north of the Barossa Valley of South Australia, extending east into New South Wales.

Roditis – White grape variety of Greece, known for fresh dry whites with decent acidity, often included in retsina.

rosso – Red wine, Italy.

Rosso Conero – DOC red wine made in the environs of Ancona in the Marches, Italy. Made from the Montepulciano grape, the wine can provide excellent value for money.

Ruby Cabernet – Black grape variety of California, created by crossing Cabernet Sauvignon and Carignan. Makes soft and squelchy red wine at home and in South Africa.

Rueda – DO of north-west Spain making first-class refreshing dry whites from the indigenous Verdejo grape, imported Sauvignon, and others. Exciting quality, and prices are keen.

Rully – AC of Chalonnais region of southern Burgundy, France. White wines from Chardonnay and red wines from Pinot Noir grapes. Both can be very good and substantially cheaper than their more northerly Burgundian neighbours. Pronounced 'ROO-yee'.

S

Sagrantino – Black grape variety native to Perugia, Italy. Dark, tannic wines best known in DOCG Sagrantino de Montefalco. Now also cultivated in Australia.

Saint Emilion – AC of Bordeaux, France. Centred on the romantic hill town of St Emilion, this famous sub-region makes some of the grandest red wines of France, but also some of the best-value ones. Less fashionable than the Médoc region on the opposite (west) bank of the River Gironde that bisects Bordeaux, St Emilion wines are made largely with the Merlot grape, and are relatively quick to mature. The top wines are classified *1er grand cru classé* and are madly expensive, but many more are classified respectively *grand cru classé* and *grand cru*, and these designations can be seen as a fairly trustworthy indicator of quality. There are several 'satellite' St Emilion ACs named after the villages at their centres, notably Lussac St Emilion, Montagne St Emilion and Puisseguin St Emilion. Some excellent wines are made by estates within these ACs, and at relatively affordable prices thanks to the comparatively humble status of their satellite designations.

Salento – Up-and-coming wine region of southern Italy. Many good bargain reds from local grapes including Nero d'Avola and Primitivo.

Sancerre – AC of the Loire Valley, France, renowned for flinty-fresh Sauvignon Blanc whites and rarer Pinot Noir reds and rosés.

Sangiovese – The local black grape of Tuscany, Italy, is the principal variety used for Chianti. Also planted further south in Italy and in the New World. Generic Sangiovese di Toscana can make a consoling substitute for costly Chianti.

Saumur – Town and appellation of Loire Valley, France. Characterful minerally red wines from Cabernet Franc grapes, and some whites. Sparkling wines from Chenin Blanc grapes can be good value.

Saumur-Champigny – Separate appellation for red wines from Cabernet Franc grapes of Saumur in the Loire, sometimes very good and lively.

Sauvignon Blanc – French white grape variety now grown worldwide. New Zealand has raised worldwide production values challenging the long supremacy of French ACs in Bordeaux and the Loire Valley. Chile and South Africa aspire similarly. The wines are characterised by aromas of gooseberry, peapod, fresh-cut grass, even asparagus. Flavours are often described as 'grassy' or 'nettly'.

sec – Dry wine style. French.

secco – Dry wine style. Italian.

seco – Dry wine style. Spanish.

Semillon – White grape variety originally of Bordeaux, where it is blended with Sauvignon Blanc to make fresh dry whites and, when harvested very late in the season, the ambrosial sweet whites of Barsac, Sauternes and other appellations. Even in the driest wines, the grape can be recognised from its honeyed, sweet-pineapple, even banana-like aromas. Now widely planted in Australia and Latin America, and frequently blended with Chardonnay to make dry whites, some of them interesting.

sherry – The great aperitif wine of Spain, centred on the Andalusian city of Jerez (the name 'sherry' is an English mispronunciation). There is a lot of sherry-style wine in the world, but only the authentic wine from Jerez and the neighbouring producing centres of Puerta de Santa Maria and Sanlucar de Barrameda may label their wines as such. The Spanish drink real sherry – very dry and fresh, pale in colour and served well-chilled – called fino and manzanilla, and darker but naturally dry variations called amontillado, palo cortado and oloroso.

Shiraz – Australian name for the Syrah grape. The variety is the most widely planted of any in Australia, and makes red wines of wildly varying quality, characterised by dense colour, high alcohol, spicy fruit and generous, cushiony texture.

Somontano – Wine region of north-east Spain. Name means 'under the mountains' – in this case the Pyrenees – and the region has had DO status since 1984. Much innovative winemaking here, with New World styles emerging. Some very good buys. A region to watch.

souple – French wine-tasting term that translates into English as 'supple' or even 'docile' as in 'pliable', but I understand it in the vinous context to mean muscular but soft – a wine with tannin as well as soft fruit.

Spätlese – *See* QmP.

spirity – Some wines, mostly from the New World, are made from grapes so ripe at harvest that their high alcohol content can be detected through a mildly burning sensation on the tongue, similar to the effect of sipping a spirit. Young Port wines can be detectably spirity.

spritzy – Describes a wine with a gentle sparkle. Some young wines are intended to have this elusive fizziness; in others it is a fault.

spumante – Sparkling wine of Italy. Asti Spumante is the best known, from the town of Asti in the north-west Italian province of Piemonte. Many Prosecco wines are labelled as Spumante in style. The term describes wines that are fully sparkling. Frizzante wines have a less vigorous mousse.

stalky – A useful tasting term to describe red wines with flavours that make you think the stalks from the grape bunches must have been fermented along with the must (juice). Red Loire wines and youthful claret very often have this mild astringency. In moderation it's fine, but if it dominates it probably signifies the wine is at best immature and at worst badly made.

Stellenbosch – Town and region at the heart of South Africa's wine industry. It's an hour's drive from Cape Town and the source of much of the country's cheaper wine. Some serious-quality estate wines as well.

stony – Wine-tasting term for keenly dry white wines. It's meant to indicate a wine of purity and real quality, with just the right match of fruit and acidity.

structured – Good wines are not one-dimensional, they have layers of flavour and texture. A structured wine has phases of enjoyment: the 'attack', or first impression in the mouth; the middle palate as the wine is held in the mouth; and the lingering aftertaste.

sugar – *See* residual sugar.

sulphites – Nearly all wines, barring some esoteric 'natural' types of a kind not found in supermarkets are made with the aid of preparations containing sulphur to combat diseases in the vineyards and bacterial infections in the winery. It's difficult to make wine without sulphur. Even 'organic' wines need it. Because some people are sensitive to the traces of sulphur in some wines, worldwide health authorities insist wine labels bear the warning 'Contains sulphites'.

summer fruit – Wine-tasting term intended to convey a smell or taste of soft fruits such as strawberries and raspberries – without having to commit too specifically to which.

superiore – On labels of Italian wines, this is more than an idle boast. Under DOC(G) rules, wines must qualify for the *superiore* designation by reaching one or more specified quality levels, usually a higher alcohol content or an additional period of maturation. Frascati, for example, qualifies for DOC status at 11.5 per cent alcohol, but to be classified *superiore* must have 12 per cent alcohol.

sur lie – Literally, 'on the lees'. It's a term now widely used on the labels of Muscadet wines, signifying that after fermentation has died down, the new wine has been left in the tank over the winter on the lees – the detritus of yeasts and other interesting compounds left over from the turbid fermentation process. The idea is that additional interest is imparted into the flavour of the wine.

Syrah – The noble grape of the Rhône Valley, France. Makes very dark, dense wine characterised by peppery, tarry aromas. Now planted all over southern France and farther afield. In Australia it is known as Shiraz.

T

table wine – Wine that is unfortified and of an alcoholic strength, for UK tax purposes anyway, of no more than 15 per cent. I use the term to distinguish, for example, between the red table wines of the Douro Valley in Portugal and the region's better-known fortified wine, port.

Tafelwein – Table wine, German. The humblest quality designation, which doesn't usually bode very well.

tank method – Bulk-production process for sparkling wines. Base wine undergoes secondary fermentation in a large, sealed vat rather than in individual closed bottles. Also known as the Charmat method after the name of the inventor of the process. Prosecco is made by the tank method.

Tai – White grape variety of north-east Italy, a relative of Sauvignon Blanc. Also known in Italy as Tocai Friulano or, more correctly, Friulano.

Tannat – Black grape of south-west France, notably for wines of Madiran, and lately named as the variety most beneficial to health thanks to its outstanding antioxidant content.

tannin – Well known as the film-forming, teeth-coating component in tea, tannin is a natural compound that occurs in black grape skins and acts as a natural preservative in wine. Its noticeable presence in wine is regarded as a good thing. It gives young everyday reds their dryness, firmness of flavour and backbone. And it helps high-quality reds to retain their lively fruitiness for many years. A grand Bordeaux red when first made, for example, will have purply-sweet, rich fruit and mouth-puckering tannin, but after ten years or so this will have evolved into a delectably fruity, mature wine in which the formerly parching effects of the tannin have receded almost completely, leaving the shade of 'residual tannin' that marks out a great wine approaching maturity.

Tarrango – Black grape variety of Australia.

tarry – On the whole, winemakers don't like critics to say their wines evoke the redolence of road repairs, but I can't help using this term to describe the agreeable, sweet, 'burnt' flavour that is often found at the centre of the fruit in red wines from Argentina, Italy, Portugal and South Africa in particular.

TCA – Dreaded ailment in wine, usually blamed on faulty corks. It stands for 246 *trichloroanisol* and is characterised by a horrible musty smell and flavour in the affected wine. Thanks to technological advances made by cork manufacturers in Portugal – the leading cork nation – TCA is now in retreat.

tears – The colourless alcohol in the wine left clinging to the inside of the glass after the contents have been swirled. Persistent tears (also known as 'legs') indicate a wine of good concentration.

Tempranillo – The great black grape of Spain. Along with Garnacha (Grenache in France) it makes most red Rioja and Navarra wines and, under many pseudonyms, is an important or exclusive contributor to the wines of many other regions of Spain. It is also widely cultivated in South America.

Teroldego – Black grape variety of Trentino, northern Italy. Often known as Teroldego Rotaliano after the Rotaliano region where most of the vineyards lie. Deep-coloured, assertive, green-edged red wines.

terroir – French word for 'ground' or 'soil' has mystical meaning in vineyard country. Winemakers attribute the distinct characteristics of their products, not just to the soil conditions but to the lie of the land and the prevailing (micro)climate, all within the realm of terroir. The word now frequently appears on effusive back labels asserting the unique appeal of the wine. Some critics scoff that terroir is all imagined nonsense.

tinto – On Spanish labels indicates a deeply coloured red wine. Clarete denotes a paler colour. Also Portuguese.

Toro – Quality wine region east of Zamora, Spain.

Torrontes – White grape variety of Argentina. Makes soft, dry wines often with delicious grapey-spicy aroma, similar in style to the classic dry Muscat wines of Alsace, but at more accessible prices.

Touraine – Region encompassing a swathe of the Loire Valley, France. Non-AC wines may be labelled 'Sauvignon de Touraine'.

Touriga Nacional – The most valued black grape variety of the Douro Valley in Portugal, where port is made. The name Touriga now appears on an increasing number of table wines made as sidelines by the port producers. They can be very good, with the same spirity aroma and sleek flavours of port itself, minus the fortification.

Traminer – Grape variety, the same as Gewürztraminer.

Trebbiano – The workhorse white grape of Italy. A productive variety that is easy to cultivate, it seems to be included in just about every ordinary white wine of the entire nation – including Frascati, Orvieto and Soave. It is the same grape as France's Ugni Blanc. There are, however, distinct regional variations of the grape. Trebbiano di Lugana (also known as Turbiana) makes a distinctive white in the DOC of the name, sometimes very good, while Trebbiano di Toscana makes a major contribution to the distinctly less interesting dry whites of Chianti country.

Trincadeira Preta – Portuguese black grape variety native to the port-producing vineyards of the Douro Valley (where it goes under the name Tinta Amarella). In southern Portugal, it produces dark and sturdy table wines.

trocken – 'Dry' German wine. The description does have a particular meaning under German wine law, namely that there is only a low level of unfermented sugar lingering in the wine (9 grams per litre, if you need to know), and this can leave the wine tasting rather austere.

U

Ugni Blanc – The most widely cultivated white grape variety of France and the mainstay of many a cheap dry white wine. To date it has been better known as the provider of base wine for distilling into armagnac and cognac, but lately the name has been appearing on wine labels. Technology seems to be improving the performance of the grape. The curious name is pronounced 'OON-yee', and is the same variety as Italy's ubiquitous Trebbiano.

Utiel-Requena – Region and *Denominación de Origen* of Mediterranean Spain inland from Valencia. Principally red wines from Bobal, Garnacha and Tempranillo grapes grown at relatively high altitude, between 600 and 900 metres.

V

Vacqueyras – Village of the southern Rhône Valley of France in the region better known for its generic appellation, the Côtes du Rhône. Vacqueyras can date its winemaking history all the way back to 1414, but has only been producing under its own village AC since 1991. The wines, from Grenache and Syrah grapes, can be wonderfully silky and intense, spicy and long-lived.

Valdepeñas – An island of quality production amidst the ocean of mediocrity that is Spain's La Mancha region – where most of the grapes are grown for distilling into the head-banging brandies of Jerez. Valdepeñas reds are made from a grape they call the Cencibel – which turns out to be a very close relation of the Tempranillo grape that is the mainstay of the fine but expensive red wines of Rioja. Again, like Rioja, Valdepeñas wines are matured in oak casks to give them a vanilla-rich smoothness. Among bargain reds, Valdepeñas is a name to look out for.

Valpolicella – Red wine of Verona, Italy. Good examples have ripe, cherry fruit and a pleasingly dry finish. Unfortunately, there are many bad examples of Valpolicella. Shop with circumspection. Valpolicella Classico wines, from the best vineyards clustered around the town, are more reliable. Those additionally labelled *superiore* have higher alcohol and some bottle age.

vanilla – Ageing wines in oak barrels (or, less picturesquely, adding oak chips to wine in huge concrete vats) imparts a range of characteristics including a smell of vanilla from the ethyl vanilline naturally given off by oak.

varietal – A varietal wine is one named after the grape variety (one or more) from which it is made. Nearly all everyday wines worldwide are now labelled in this way. It is salutary to contemplate that until the present wine boom began in the 1980s, wines described thus were virtually unknown outside Germany and one or two quirky regions of France and Italy.

vegan-friendly – My informal way of noting that a wine is claimed to have been made not only with animal-product-free finings (*see* vegetarian wine) but without any animal-related products whatsoever, such as livestock manure in the vineyards.

vegetal – A tasting note definitely open to interpretation. It suggests a smell or flavour reminiscent less of fruit (apple, pineapple, strawberry and the like) than of something leafy or even root based. Some wines are evocative (to some tastes) of beetroot, cabbage or even unlikelier vegetable flavours – and these characteristics may add materially to the attraction of the wine.

vegetarian wine – Wines labelled 'suitable for vegetarians' have been made without the assistance of animal products for 'fining' – clarifying – before bottling. Gelatine, egg whites, isinglass from fish bladders and casein from milk are among the items shunned, usually in favour of bentonite, an absorbent clay first found at Benton in the US state of Montana.

Verdejo – White grape of the Rueda region in north-west Spain. It can make superbly perfumed crisp dry whites of truly distinctive character and has helped make Rueda one of the best white-wine sources of Europe. No relation to Verdelho.

Verdelho – Portuguese grape variety once mainly used for a medium-dry style of Madeira, also called Verdelho, but now rare. The vine is now prospering in Australia, where it can make well-balanced dry whites with fleeting richness and lemon-lime acidity.

Verdicchio – White grape variety of Italy best known in the DOC zone of Castelli di Jesi in the Adriatic wine region of the Marches. Dry white wines once known for little more than their naff amphora-style bottles but now gaining a reputation for interesting, herbaceous flavours of recognisable character.

Vermentino – White grape variety principally of Italy, especially Sardinia. Makes florally scented soft dry whites.

Vieilles vignes – Old vines. Many French producers like to claim on their labels that the wine within is from vines of notable antiquity. While it's true that vines don't produce useful grapes for the first few years after planting, it is uncertain whether vines of much greater age – say 25 years plus – than others actually make better fruit. There are no regulations governing the use of the term, so it's not a reliable indicator anyway.

Vin de France – In effect, the new Vin de Table of France's morphing wine laws. The label may state the vintage (if all the wine in the blend does come from a single year's harvest) and the grape varieties that constitute the wine. It may not state the region of France from which the wine originates.

vin de liqueur – Sweet style of white wine mostly from the Pyrenean region of south-westernmost France, made by adding a little spirit to the new wine before it has fermented out, halting the fermentation and retaining sugar.

vin de pays – 'Country wine' of France. Introduced in 1968 and regularly revised ever since, it's the wine-quality designation between basic Vin de France and AOC/AOP. Although being superseded by the more recently introduced IGP (*qv*), there are more than 150 producing areas permitted to use the description vin de pays. Some vin de pays areas are huge: the Vin de Pays d'Oc (referencing the Languedoc region) covers much of the Midi and Provence. Plenty of wines bearing this humble designation are of astoundingly high quality and certainly compete with New World counterparts for interest and value. *See* Indication Géographique Protégée.

vin de table – Formerly official designation of generic French wine, now used only informally. *See* Vin de France.

vin doux naturel – Sweet, mildly fortified wine of southern France. A little spirit is added during the winemaking process, halting the fermentation by killing the yeast before it has consumed all the sugars – hence the pronounced sweetness of the wine.

vin gris – Rosé wine from Provence.

Vinho de mesa – 'Table wine' of Portugal.

Vino da tavola – The humblest official classification of Italian wine. Much ordinary plonk bears this designation, but the bizarre quirks of Italy's wine laws dictate that some of that country's finest wines are also classed as mere vino da tavola (table wine). If an expensive Italian wine is labelled as such, it doesn't mean it will be a disappointment.

Vino de la Tierra – Generic classification for regional wines, Spain. Abbreviates to VdT.

Vino de mesa – 'Table wine' of Spain. Usually very ordinary.

vintage – The grape harvest. The year displayed on bottle labels is the year of the harvest. Wines bearing no date have been blended from the harvests of two or more years.

Viognier – A white grape variety once exclusive to the northern Rhône Valley in France where it makes expensive Condrieu. Now, Viognier is grown more widely, in North and South America as well as elsewhere in France, and occasionally produces soft, marrowy whites that echo the grand style of Condrieu itself. The Viognier is now commonly blended with Shiraz in red winemaking in Australia and South Africa. It does not dilute the colour and is confidently believed by highly experienced winemakers to enhance the quality. Steve Webber, in charge of winemaking at the revered De Bortoli estates in the Yarra Valley region of Victoria, Australia, puts between two and five per cent Viognier in with some of his Shiraz wines. 'I think it's the perfume,' he told me. 'It gives some femininity to the wine.'

Viura – White grape variety of Rioja, Spain. Also widely grown elsewhere in Spain under the name Macabeo. Wines have a blossomy aroma and are dry, but sometimes soft at the expense of acidity.

Vouvray – AC of the Loire Valley, France, known for still and sparkling dry white wines and sweet, still whites from late-harvested grapes. The wines, all from Chenin Blanc grapes, have a unique capacity for unctuous softness combined with lively freshness – an effect best portrayed in the demi-sec (slightly sweet) wines, which can be delicious and keenly priced.

Vranac – Black grape variety of the Balkans known for dense colour and tangy-bitter edge to the flavour. Best enjoyed in situ.

W

weight – In an ideal world the weight of a wine is determined by the ripeness of the grapes from which it has been made. In some cases the weight is determined merely by the quantity of sugar added during the production process. A good, genuine wine described as having weight is one in which there is plenty of alcohol and 'extract' – colour and flavour from the grapes. Wine enthusiasts judge weight by swirling the wine in the glass and then examining the 'legs' or 'tears' left clinging to the inside of the glass after the contents have subsided. Alcohol gives these runlets a dense, glycerine-like condition, and if they cling for a long time, the wine is deemed to have weight – a very good thing in all honestly made wines.

Winzergenossenschaft – One of the many very lengthy and peculiar words regularly found on labels of German wines. This means a winemaking co-operative. Many excellent German wines are made by these associations of growers.

woody – A subjective tasting note. A faintly rank odour or flavour suggesting the wine has spent too long in cask.

X

Xarel-lo – One of the main grape varieties for cava, the sparkling wine of Spain.

Xinomavro – Black grape variety of Greece. It retains its acidity even in the very hot conditions that prevail in many Greek vineyards, where harvests tend to over-ripen and make cooked-tasting wines. Modern winemaking techniques are capable of making well-balanced wines from Xinomavro.

Y

Yecla – Town and DO wine region of eastern Spain, close to Alicante, making interesting, strong-flavoured red and white wines, often at bargain prices.

yellow – White wines are not white at all, but various shades of yellow – or, more poetically, gold. Some white wines with opulent richness even have a flavour I cannot resist calling yellow – reminiscent of butter.

Z

Zibibbo – Sicilian white grape variety synonymous with north African variety Muscat of Alexandria. Scantily employed in sweet winemaking, and occasionally for drier styles.

Zierfandler – Esoteric white grape of Thermenregion, Austria. Aromatic dry wines and rare late-harvest sweet wines.

Zinfandel – Black grape variety of California. Makes brambly reds, some of which can age very gracefully, and 'blush' whites – actually pink, because a little of the skin colour is allowed to leach into the must. The vine is also planted in Australia and South America. The Primitivo of southern Italy is said to be a related variety, but makes a very different kind of wine.

Zweigelt – Black grape of Austria making juicy red wines for drinking young. Some wines are aged in oak to make interesting, heftier long-keepers.

Index